86

MAIN STREETS

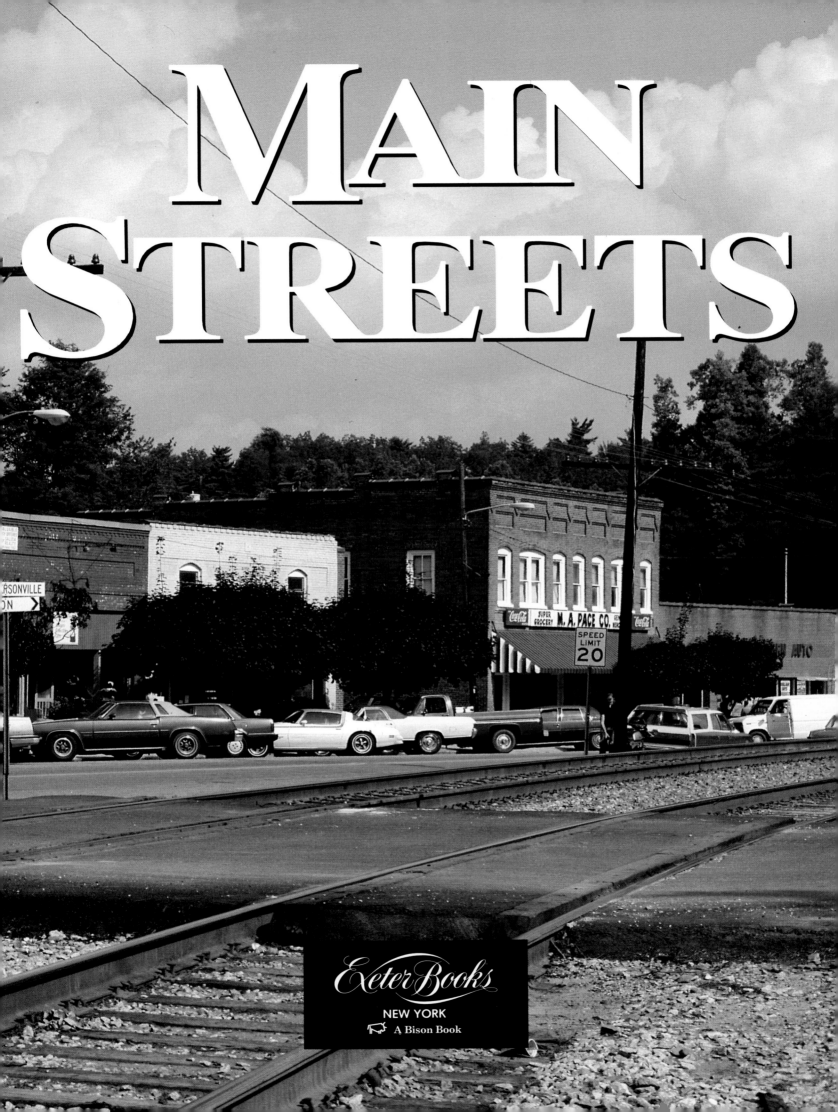

MAIN STREETS

Exeter Books

NEW YORK

A Bison Book

ISBN 0-7917-0186-7

Printed in Hong Kong

Pages 2–3: The main street of Saluda, North Carolina, where Thompson's market still competes with the old Pace store down the block, and those lazy old clouds mosey around the patches of sunshine in the blue sky above. Every so often, there's thunder—from the wheels of old Number Nine, as that aged but still awesome freight train gives a blast from its horn as it passes through town.

Below: Main Street does not have to have stop lights, pavement or even two sides! Main Street can take on a variety of forms, and the folks in Meadowdale, Wyoming, are no doubt just as plain old proud of their main street—shown here—as the big city folks are, 'down south' in Rawlins.

PHOTO CREDITS

Alaska Division of Tourism 146–147 (both), 148–149
Alyeska Pipeline Service Company 144, 145
Harkishan S Biring 162–163, 182–183 (both)
Canada Tourism 23, 82–83
  Bob Anderson 150
  Mike Beedel 150–151
  Drie/Meir 14, 15, 26–27, 142–143, 154, 158
  Pat Morrow 154–155
  Bruce Paton 152–153
  Doug Walker 96
The Corn Palace 97
© Tom Debolski 111 (bottom)
© Ruth DeJauregui 1, 6, 28–29 (both), 103, 184–185
Florida Department of Commerce, Division of Tourism
  30–31, 46–47 (both)
Four By Five 101, 107
Georgia Department of Industry and Trade 34–35,
  38–39 (both), 40–41, 44–45, 48, 53
© George W Hamlin 2–3, 54–55, 56–57
Girl Scouts of America 126
© Nils Huxtable 93
Illinois Department of Commerce and Community
  Affairs 65 (bottom), 68–69 (both), 76–77
Rozaline K Johnson 192
Kentucky Department of Travel Development 32, 49
  (top), 50–51 (both)
© Kerry Kirkland 114–115
Louisiana Office of Tourism 41, 45, 49 (bottom), 52,
  54, 55 (both), 58–59 (both)
© Reverend MJ McPike Collection 108–109, 124–125,
  132–133, 134, 137, 140–141, 164, 165, 178–179
Maine Division of Tourism 27
  Joseph Devenney 21
Manitoba Culture, Heritage and Recreation
  Communication Advisory Service 84–85, 86–87, 90
Massachusetts Division of Tourism 7, 20

Mississippi Department of Economic Development 33,
  34
Montana Travel Promotion 116–117, 123, 129, 136
Nebraska Department of Economic Development 87
New York State Department of Commerce 10, 11, 16,
  17, 24
Oklahoma Tourism 102, 104–105, 106
Pennsylvania Bureau of Travel Development 18–19
  (both)
Salsbury/Ziglar 8–9
Smithsonian Institution 13
South Dakota Department of Tourism 92–93, 94–95
  (both), 96–97
Southern Pacific Railroad 54 (both)
Travel Alberta 113, 120–121
Vermont Travel Division 12–13, 22–23, 25
Washington State Tourism Division 158–159, 160, 161,
  166–167 (both), 172–173
West Virginia Tourism Division 60–61 (both)
Wisconsin Division of Tourism 62–63, 66–67 (both),
  68–69, 70–71, 74–75 (both), 80
Wyoming Travel Commission 4–5, 88–89, 90–91,
  138–139
©Bill Yenne 15, 36, 37, 42–43, 64, 65 (top), 72–73,
  74–75 (both), 81, 82, 98–99, 100, 110–111, 111
  (top), 112, 116, 118–119, 122–123, 126–127, 128,
  130–131, 134–135, 138–139, 140–141, 156–157,
  168–169, 170–171 (both), 174–175 (both), 176, 177,
  180–181, 184 (both), 186–187, 188–189 (all), 190,
  191

Designed by Ruth DeJauregui

Edited and captioned by Timothy Jacobs

**Photographs selected by Ruth DeJauregui and
  Bill Yenne**

CONTENTS

INTRODUCTION

It was the heart and the soul of my home town, the street we called 'Main.' It defined the town and served as the dividing line between those two ambiguous subcultures to the east and west—which to outsiders were identical, but to those of us who lived there, made all the difference in the world. We west-siders always felt just a little superior—a little better—but I'm sure those people on the alien east side felt the same about us too.

Main Street, however, was the melting pot. East met west in its department stores and banks. Here were the toy stores of my childhood and the record stores of my youth. On North Main—across the tracks—were the taverns of my rites of passage to adulthood, and on the corner was a place of still more transformation—the church where I, my folks and my little sister went weekly—and which I took more seriously as I grew older.

I remember when they put the stoplights in on Main Street—the rites of passage for the street upon which I'd experienced my own. I remember also the coming and going of the movie house: Disney or DeMille at the matinee; the era of disuse; the transformation to an 'art film' theater. The life of a street is told in the microcosm of that single building just as the street itself is a microcosm of the heart and soul of the culture of our continent.

A rose by any other name would still smell as sweet, just as a 'main' street by any other name is still the centerpiece of its respective town. In my rambles across the land, I've kept a page in my mental notebook to log the variety of names with which this street has been endowed. Main is quite simply the most common, of course, followed by the names of respective states, counties and founding fathers. In Columbia Falls, this vital trunk is called Nucleus Avenue, clearly among the most creative appellations.

As our towns and small cities have grown over these recent years, we have seen their core—as defined by Main Street—face competition from a new phenomena, the 'mall.' This sprawling monster skulks at the distant edge of our towns—a cowardly beast that saps our Main Street's lifeblood without daring to look it in the eye. Despite this competitor, Main Street lives and breathes for the generations of today as it did in my time.

Like the theater that now shows 'films' instead of movies, the old soda fountain now is adorned with ferns and the menu, whose centerpiece was once grilled American cheese on white bread, now offers avocado and alfalfa sprouts on bread that has nine grains. I remember when bread was made with wheat and when cows ate alfalfa, but this evolution is part of Main Street's ability to adapt to changing times. I can recall, and now I can understand, my grandfather's chagrin on the day they started putting parking meters on Main Street.

The enduring nature of Main Street is quite simply that it does endure—in our hearts and memories, and in those of generations yet to come.

—*William Patrick Jennings*
Main Street
September, 1987

At right: One of the unchanging aspects of Main Street is the presence of the church on the corner. Here, a timeless scene unfolds as a mother, with her infant and the family pet, pauses to meditate on a stately house of worship in this Berkshire County, Massachusetts town. *Below:* Another kind of timelessness beckons in this view down West Texas Street in Fairfield, California.

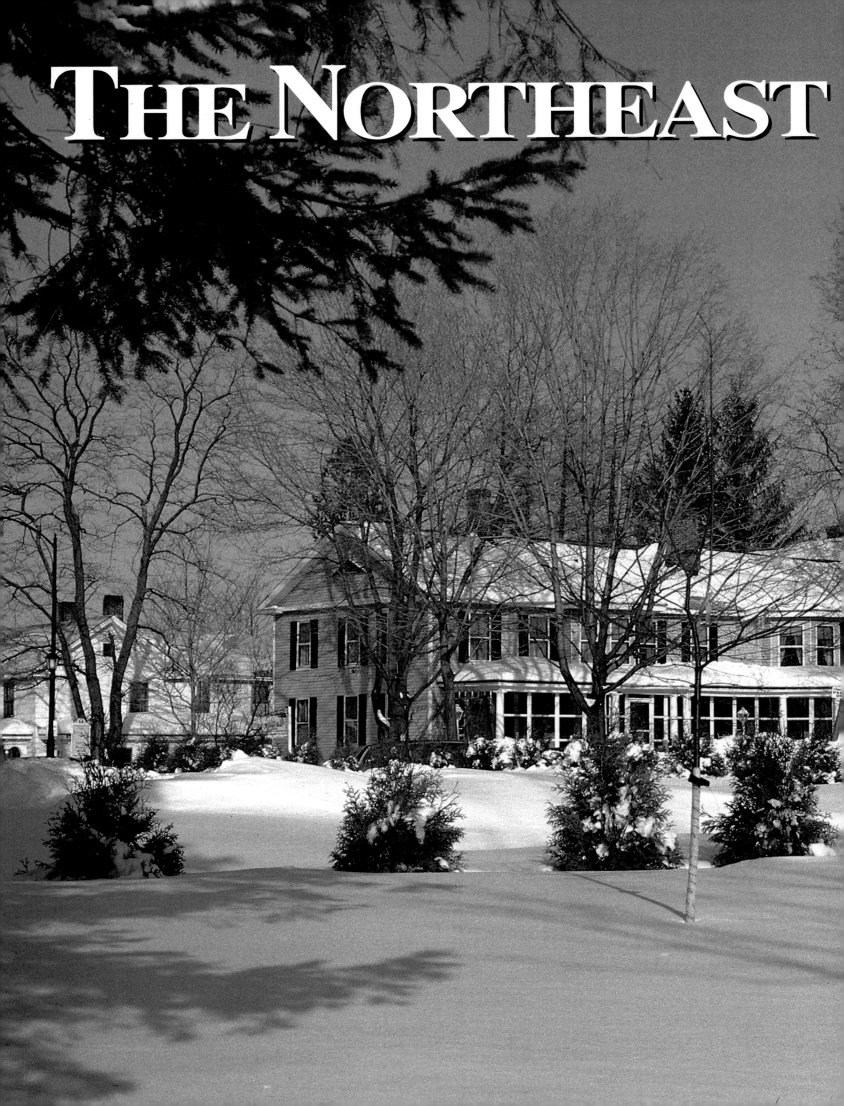

THE NORTHEAST

from
THE HOMECOMING OF THE BRIDE

Sarah Greenleaf, of eighteen years,
   Stepped lightly her bridegroom's boat within,
Waving mid-river, through smiles and tears,
   A farewell back to her kith and kin.
With her sweet blue eyes and her new gold gown,
   She sat by her stalwart lover's side—
Oh, never was brought to Haverhill town
   By land or water so fair a bride.
Glad as the glad autumnal weather,
   The Indian summer so soft and warm,
They walked through the golden woods together,
   His arm the girdle about her form.

They passed the dam and the gray gristmill,
   Whose walls with the jar of grinding shook,
And crossed, for the moment awed and still,
   The haunted bridge of the Country Brook.
The great oaks seemed on Job's Hill crown
   To wave in welcome their branches strong,
And an upland streamlet came rippling down
   Over root and rock, like a bridal song.

—John Greenleaf Whittier

Previous page: The cross-town traveler in Lenox, Massachusetts could stop for tea—and other accomodations—at the Village Inn, shown here in the thick of the New England winter. In small towns throughout eastern New York, historic sites such as the Old Dutch Church *at left* and Philipsburg Manor *(above)* invite the casual explorer to leave the car and linger awhile—and perhaps to fall into a reverie of what *Grandma's mother's* home town was like.

THE TEACHER

Lord, who am I to teach the way
To little children day by day,
So prone myself to go astray?

I teach them KNOWLEDGE, but I know
How faint they flicker and how low
The candles of my knowledge glow.

I teach them POWER to will and do,
But only now to learn anew
My own great weakness through and through.

I teach them LOVE for all mankind
And all God's creatures, but I find
My love comes lagging far behind.

Lord, if their guide I still must be,
Oh, let the little children see
The teacher leaning hard on Thee.

—*Leslie Pinckney Hill*

At left: It's 10:10 on an autumn morning, by the clock on the vigilant-looking steeple of the old church on Main Street in Stowe, Vermont. *Above:* Great Grandpa attended a tiny one room school like this. The acoutrements of learning in evidence here reveal a different scale of values than is currently in educational vogue. Though dear old Dad talked of *Grandpa* in terms of what he learned from him, Grandpa was heard to say that the smartest man he'd ever known was *his* father.

SEA FEVER

I must go down to the seas again, to the lonely sea and the sky,
And all I ask is a tall ship and a star to steer her by;
And the wheel's kick and the wind's song and the white sail's
  shaking,
And a gray mist on the sea's face, and a gray dawn breaking.

I must go down to the seas again, for the call of the running
  tide
Is a wild call and a clear call that may not be denied;
And all I ask is a windy day with the white clouds flying.
And the flung spray and the blown spume, and the sea-gulls
  crying.

I must go down to the seas again, to the vagrant gipsy life,
To the gull's way and the whale's way where the wind's like
  a whetted knife;
And all I ask is a merry yarn from a laughing fellow-rover
And quiet sleep and a sweet dream when the long trip's
  over.

—*John Masefield*

Above: Indian Harbour is a main street for the residents of Peggy's Cove, Nova Scotia—many of whom are either fishermen or gulls like the one *at right.* Any street in Lunenberg, Nova Scotia would surely bring you to that town's historic harbor *(at left),* where lobstermen ply their traditional trade.

THE THINGS THAT MAKE A SOLDIER GREAT

The things that make a soldier great and send
    him out to die,
To face the flaming cannon's mouth nor ever
    question why,
Are lilacs by a little porch, the row of tulips
    red,
The peonies and pansies, too, the old petunia bed,
The grass plot where his children play, the roses
    on the wall:
'Tis these that make a soldier great. He's fighting
    for them all.

'Tis not the pomp and pride of kings that make
    a soldier brave;
'Tis not allegiance to the flag that over him may
    wave;
For soldiers never fight so well on land or on
    the foam
As when behind the cause they see the little
    place called home.
Endanger but that humble street whereon his
    children run,
You make a soldier of the man who never bore
    a gun.

What is it through the battle smoke the valiant
    soldier sees?
The little garden far away, the budding apple
    trees,
The little patch of ground back there, the children
    at their play,
Perhaps a tiny mound behind the simple church
    of gray.
The golden thread of courage isn't linked to
    the castle dome
But to the spot, where'er it be—the humble spot
    called home.

—*Edgar A Guest*

Above: This Revolutionary War parade is one of many such events that take place on Independence Day in the towns and villages of the historic state of New York. *At* *right:* A celebrant in Revolutionary military garb sizes up the windage of this vintage cannon, which was once a fearsome weapon in the service of any foe.

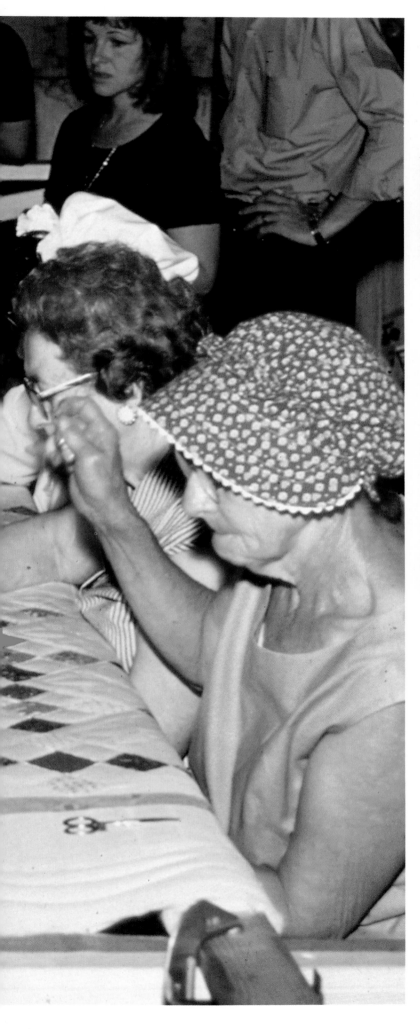

OUR CLUB

Our club is just a friendly band
  Of common folk whose aims are high—
To love and serve our native land,
  To greet our Master in the sky.

We long to make the whole world bright,
  Our interests are both far and near;
To shun the wrong, to do the right,
  We try to teach our children dear.

We're just a joyous little band
  Of old-time friends, and new ones too;
United, let us take this stand,
  To do our best and carry through.

            —*Sylvia Dillavou Barclay*

At left: These ladies enact an old tradition in a quilting bee, organized as a demonstration at the Kutztown Folk Festival, in Pennsylvania's beautiful Pennsylvania Dutch country. The little girl *above*, munching so intently on her funnel cake, may herself one day become a carrier of such tradition—if she pays close attention. Note the Pennsylvania Dutch designs on her hat.

from
MY LOST YOUTH

Often I think of the beautiful town
   That is seated by the sea;
Often in thought go up and down
The pleasant streets of that dear old town,
   And my youth comes back to me.
     And a verse of a Lapland song
     Is haunting my memory still:
     'A boy's will is the wind's will,
And the thoughts of youth are long, long thoughts.'

I can see the shadowy lines of its trees,
   And catch, in sudden gleams,
The sheen of the far-surrounding seas,
And islands that were the Hesperides
   Of all my boyish dreams.
     And the burden of that old song,
     It murmurs and whispers still:
     'A boy's will is the wind's will,
And the thoughts of youth are long, long thoughts.'

I remember the black wharves and the slips,
   And the sea-tides tossing free;
And sailors with bearded lips,
And the beauty and mystery of the ships,
   And the magic of the sea.
     And the voice of that wayward song
     Is singing and saying still:
     'A boy's will is the wind's will,
And the thoughts of youth are long, long thoughts'

There are things of which I may not speak,
   There are dreams that cannot die;
There are thoughts that make the strong heart weak,
And bring a pallor into the cheek,
   And a mist before the eye.
     And the words of that fatal song
     Come over me like a chill:
     'A boy's will is the wind's will,
And the thoughts of youth are long, long thoughts.'

Strange to me now are the forms I meet
   When I visit the dear old town;
But the native air is pure and sweet,
And the trees that o'ershadow each well-known street,
   As they balance up and down,
     Are singing the beautiful song,
     Are sighing and whispering still:
     'A boy's will is the wind's will,
And the thoughts of youth are long, long thoughts.'

—Henry Wadsworth Longfellow

At left: This water-borne main street is the harbor at Rockport, Massachusetts, which has seen the coming and going of generations of Rockport fishermen. Also soaked in brine is the history of Camden, Maine *(above)*, whose pristine and classic church-at-the-center-of-town appearance includes a harbor full of boats which ply the fierce Atlantic, whose pilots are—they say 'of necessity'—'prayin' men.'

from
MY RUTHERS

I tell you what I'd ruther do—
    Ef I only had my ruthers—
I'd ruther work when I wanted to
    Than be bossed round by others—
        I'd ruther kindo' git the swing
        O' what was *needed* first, I jing!
        Afore I *sweat* at anything!
    Ef I only had my ruthers—
In fact I'd aim to be the same
    With all men as my brothers;
And they'd all be the same with me—
    Ef I only had my ruthers.

The poor 'ud git their dues *sometimes*—
    Ef I only had my ruthers—
And be paid *dollars* 'stid o' *dimes*,
    Fer children, wives and mothers:
        Their boy that slaves; their girl that sews—
        Fer *others*—not herself, God knows—
        The grave's *her* only change of clothes!
        Ef I only had my ruthers,
They'd all have 'stuff' and time enough
    To answer one another's
Appealin' prayer fer lovin' care—
    Ef I only had my ruthers.

They'd be few folks would ask fer trust,
    Ef I only had my ruthers,
And blame few business-men to bust
    Theirselves, or hearts of others:
        Big Guns that come here durin' Fair-
        Week could put up jest anywhere,
        And find a full-and-plenty there,
    Ef I only had my ruthers:
The rich and great would 'sociate
    With all their lowly brothers,
Feelin' *we* done the honorin'—
    Ef I only had my ruthers.

           —*Benj F Johnson, of Boone*
           (James Whitcomb Riley)

At left: The parade is on in Montpelier, Vermont, when the Montpelier Theater Guild hits the asphalt. Colorful as any county fair, these folks exhibit integrity of costume— no snubbing, and no one-upmanship here: 'At yer leisure, sir.' Surely the queen of any parade, this friendly thespian *(above)* wears a sunshiney costume, which she may or may not have sewn herself.

from
DECORATION DAY ON THE PLACE

It's lonesome—sorto' lonesome—it's a *Sund'y-day*, to me,
It 'pears-like—more'n any day I nearly ever see!
Yet, with the Stars and Stripes above, a-flutterin' in the air,
On ev'ry Soldier's grave I'd love to lay a lily there.

They say, though, Decoration Days is ginerly observed
Most *ev'rywhares*—especially by soldier-boys that's served.
But me and Mother's never went—we seldom git away—
In pint o'fact, we're *allus* home on *Decoration Day*.

They say the old boys marches through the streets in columns grand,
A-follerin' the old war-tunes they're playin' on the band—
And citizuns all jinin' in—and little children, too—
All marchin' under shelter of the old Red White and Blue.

Oh! can't they hear the bugle and the rattle of the drum?
Ain't they no way under heavens they can rickollect us some?
Ain't they no way we can coax 'em, through the roses, jest to say
They know that ev'ry day on earth's their Decoration Day?

We've tried that—me and Mother—whare Elias takes his rest,
In the orchard—in his uniform, and hands across his brest,
And the flag he died fer, smilin' and a-ripplin' in the breeze
Above his grave—and over that—*the robin in the trees!*

And yit it's lonesome—lonesome! It's a *Sund'y-day*, to *me*,
It 'pears-like—more'n any day I nearly ever see!
Still, with the Stars and Stripes above, a-flutterin' in the air,
On ev'ry Soldier's grave I'd love to lay a lily there.

—*Benj F Johnson, of Boone*
(James Whitcomb Riley)

Above: These soldiers take a wary stance at a Revolutionary War encampment in New Windsor, New York—some 200 years after the war itself took place! *At right:* The American Legion fife and drum unit of Claremont, New Hampshire marches down the main street of Montpelier, Vermont in an interstate Memorial Day parade.

THE TIDE RISES, THE TIDE FALLS

The tide rises, the tide falls,
The twilight darkens, the curlew calls;
Along the sea-sands damp and brown
The traveller hastens toward the town,
    And the tide rises, the tide falls.

Darkness settles on roofs and walls,
But the sea, the sea in the darkness calls;
The little waves, with their soft, white hands,
Efface the footprints in the sands,
    And the tide rises, the tide falls.

—*Henry Wadswsorth Longfellow*

At left: The weathered old docks at Ecum Secum, Nova Scotia—strewn with floats, and the playground of hundreds of gulls—are a familiar scene to anyone who has any serious business in this old seaside town. *Above:* Presiding over the sea at the end of town in Portland, Maine, this old and well cared-for lighthouse is a veritable emblem of the cleanly, astute ways of its seaside home. The lighthouse is the lighthouse keeper's sacred trust, for over the years, many a sailor has found safe harbor by this steadfast beacon.

from
THE OLD BURYING GROUND

Our vales are sweet with fern and rose,
  Our hills are maple-crowned;
But not from them our fathers chose
  The village burying ground.

The hard and thorny path they kept
  From beauty turned aside;
Nor missed they over those who slept
  The grace to life denied.

Yet still the wilding flowers would blow,
  The golden leaves would fall,
The seasons come, the seasons go,
  And God be good to all.

Above the graves the blackberry hung
  In bloom and green its wreath,
And harebells swung as if they rung
  The chimes of peace beneath.

The beauty Nature loves to share,
  The gifts she hath for all,
The common light, the common air,
  Overcrept the graveyard's wall.

Secure on God's all-tender heart
  Alike rest great and small;
Why fear to lose our little part,
  When He is pledged for all?

O fearful heart and troubled brain!
  Take hope and strength from this—
That Nature never hints in vain,
  Nor prophesies amiss.

Her wild birds sing the same sweet stave,
  Her lights and airs are given
Alike to playground and the grave;
  And over both is Heaven.

—*John Greenleaf Whittier*

And at the very edge of town, Main Street skirts the old graveyard. *Above:* This flower-bedecked plaque nestles peacefully in the dew, and the classic memorial garden *at right* is complete with a tree-shaded mausoleum, and a variety of elegantly carved monuments dedicated to the memory of those who shaped Main Street's past.

NEITZEL
FRANK E. NEITZEL
1831 — 1913.
JOHANNA NEITZEL
1831 — 1919
SARAH V. MAYHOOD
1857 — 1912
FATHER
AMBROSE JOHNSON
DECEMBER 22, 1859
MAY 23, 1927
TOBY JOHNSON
O'DELL

THE SOUTH

A SONG OF THANKS

For the bounty which the rich soil yields,
For the cooling dews and refreshing rains,
For the sun which ripens the golden grains,
For the bearded wheat and the fattened swine,
For the stalled ox and the fruitful vine,
For the tubers large and cotton white,
For the kid and the lambkin frisk and blithe,
For the swan which floats near the riverbanks—
Lord God of Hosts, we give Thee thanks!

For the lowly cot and the mansion fair,
For the peace and plenty together share,
For the Hand which guides us from above,
For Thy tender mercies, abiding love,
For the blessed home with its children gay,
For returnings of Thanksgiving Day,
For the bearing toils and the sharing cares,
We lift up our hearts in our songs and our prayers—
From the Gulf and the Lakes to the Oceans' banks—
Lord God of Hosts, we give Thee thanks!

—*Edward Smyth Jones*

Previous page: It could be almost anywhere, with a smiling mother pushing her two children on a swing. Of course the sun, sand and deep blue sky betray this as Seaside—a small resort community on the Florida coast. And what father hasn't paused in the park to consider, with his son, where all the goodness we call life comes from? This Kentucky man *(above)* is doing just that, in spirit similar to the congregation of the Handsboro Presbyterian Church *(at right)* in Pass Christian, Mississippi.

MY MOTHER'S QUILT

My mother cut the pieces,
And sewed them one by one
Into a beautiful pattern,
Until the quilt was done.

Some were bright and glowing,
Others a duller shade,
But all brought out the colors
Of flowers, down in our glade.

I see her face before me
With eyes and cheeks aglow,
Threading her needle swiftly,
Which made the quilt grow.

She sewed the pieces together,
Then placed them on the white,
And beneath her nimble fingers
Several blocks were done by night.

At last the quilt was finished,
Quilted in stitches fine,
And breathlessly we both looked on
That handiwork of—time.

—*Margaret Rushmer*

Above: The old Antique shop nestles to the left of the historic WJ Hogan building—
built in 1888—in picturesque downtown Natchez, Mississippi. Another milestone on
the main street of time is the care and precision the elderly craftswoman *at right* dedi-
cates to the making of a quilt in her hometown in rural Georgia.

RIDING TO TOWN

When labor is light and the morning is fair,
I find it a pleasure beyond all compare
To hitch up my nag and go hurrying down
And take Katie May for a ride into town;
    For bumpety-bump goes the wagon,
        But tra-la-la-la our lay.
There's joy in a song as we rattle along
    In the light of the glorious day.

A coach would be fine, but a spring wagon's good;
My jeans are a match for Kate's gingham and hood;
The hills take us up and the vales take us down,
But what matters that? We are riding to town,
    And bumpety-bump goes the wagon,
        But tra-la-la-la sing we.
There's never a care may live in the air
    That is filled with the breath of our glee.

And after we've started, there's naught can repress
The thrill of our hearts in their wild happiness;
The heavens may smile or the heavens may frown,
And it's all one to us when we're riding to town.
    For bumpety-bump goes the wagon,
        But tra-la-la-la we shout,
For our hearts they are clear and there's nothing to fear,
    And we've never a pain nor a doubt.

The wagon is weak and the roadway is rough,
And tho' it is long it is not long enough,
For mid all my ecstasies this is the crown
To sit beside Katie and ride into town,
    When bumpety-bump goes the wagon,
        But tra-la-la-la our song;
And if I had my way, I'd be willing to pay
    If the road could be made twice as long.

—*Paul Lawrence Dunbar*

Many a Beau and his Katie May drove down the unpaved thoroughfare *above* in the days of of long ago. This is actually a reproduction of a colonial main street in histori-cally important Williamsburg, Virginia—as is the beautiful building *at right*, which Katie and her Beau would have seen, once they got to town.

PURPOSE

Not for the sake of the gold,
   Not for the sake of the fame,
Not for the prize would I hold
   Any ambition or aim:
I would be brave and be true
Just for the good I can do.

I would be useful on earth,
   Serving some purpose or cause,
Doing some labor of worth,
   Giving no thought to applause.
Thinking less of the gold or the fame
Than the joy and the thrill of the game.

Medals their brightness may lose,
   Fame be forgotten or fade,
Any reward we may choose
   Leaves the account still unpaid.
But little real happiness lies
In fighting alone for a prize.

—*Edgar A Guest*

Above: A craftsman plies cane and slatting to weave an intricate basket at an outdoor site in Hiawassee, Georgia. *At right:* This crafts fair at Prater's Mill in North West Point, Georgia reflects the civic good spirit which makes towns and villages 'communities.'

CANOE RIDES
IN BACK CORNER

JOHNS BAR-B-Q

N.W. MIDDLE
SCHOOL
SOUP BOOTH

N.W.M.S. FOOD BOOTH

I HEAR AMERICA SINGING

I hear America singing, the varied carols I hear,
Those of mechanics, each one singing his as it should be
  blithe and strong
The carpenter singing his as he measures his plank or beam,
The mason singing his as he makes ready for work, or leaves
  off work,
The boatman singing what belongs to him in his boat, the
  deckhand singing on the steamboat deck,
The shoemaker singing as he sits on his bench, the hatter
  singing as he stands,
The wood-cutter's song, the ploughboy's on his way in the
  morning, or at noon intermission or at sundown,
The delicious singing of the mother, or of the young wife at
  work, or of the girl sewing or washing,
Each singing what belongs to him or her and to none else,
The day what belongs to the day—at night the party of young
  fellows, robust, friendly,
Singing with open mouths their strong melodious songs.

—*Walt Whitman*

The music's going strong at Prater's Mill *(at left)*, and all across the countryside, the resonances sound; not just one, but two guitars and a violin are ringing out—and way over at the Sawmill Days Celebration *(above)* in Fisher, Louisiana, folks are starting to pick and pluck and sing a tune right out on the general store's front porch!

"Cline Garrett - Board Splittin'"

from
SONGS OF LABOR

Let foplings sneer, let fools deride,
   Ye heed no idle scorner;
Free hands and hearts are still your pride,
   And duty done your honor.
Ye dare to trust, for honest fame,
   The jury Time empanels,
And leave to truth each noble name
   Which glorifies your annals.

The red brick to the mason's hand,
   The brown earth to the tiller's,
The show in yours shall wealth command,
   Like fairy Cinderella's!
As they who shunned the household maid
   Beheld the crown upon her,
So all shall see your toil repaid
   With heart and home and honor.

Then let the toast be freely quaffed,
   In water cool and brimming—
'All honor to the good old Craft,
   Its merry men and women!'

          —John Greenleaf Whittier

Previous page: That bottled elixir known as Coca-Cola was invented here, at the Biedenharn Candy Company, in little old Natchez, Mississippi—population 22,015. *At left:* The honorable work continues: a boy looks on and learns as an experienced hand splits shakes for shingles the old-fashioned way—in Hiawassee, Georgia. *Above:* Another level of astuteness is displayed by this weathered cane worker at the Pecan Festival in Colfax, Louisiana.

from
HYMN

Oh, none in all the world before
 Were ever glad as we!
We're free on Florida's shore,
 We're all at home and free.

Thou Friend and Helper of the poor,
 Who suffered for our sake,
To open every prison door,
 And every yoke to break!

Bend low Thy pitying face and mild,
 And help us sing and pray;
The hand that blessed the little child,
 Upon our foreheads lay.

We hear no more the driver's horn,
 No more the whip we fear,
This holy day that saw Thee born
 Was never half so dear.

We praise Thee in our songs today,
 To Thee in prayer we call,
Make swift the feet and straight the way
 Of freedom unto all.

Come again, O blessed Lord!
 Come walking on the sea!
And let the mainlands hear the word
 That sets the island free!

—John Greenleaf Whittier

Above: These rugged old immigrants at Tarpon Springs, Florida, are weary but grateful for the abundance of a day at sea, by which they, as their fathers did before them, make their living. *At right:* The open decks on these houses are known as 'widow's walks,' where the wives of fishermen await sight of their husbands' vessels as they return across the sea to this Florida island.

CRAFTSFOLK

Near the old sidestreet, the ancient guild workers
still ply their trades as they did long ago,
the wind in the porch eves tugs at their makings
and still the old craftsfolk saw, shape and sew.

And let's hear a tune for the ancestral workers
who strove with their hands long before the machine;
whose fingers worked lightly with uncanny deftness,
whose hands built the strongest and best for the queen.

And many's the gent, and many's the poorman
whose delight is enflamed by a well-woven chair,
whose eyes still limn lively a neat-carven mantle,
whose thanks are profound to the makers who care!

—*Andrew Jacobs*

At left: Care and precision is needed for the proper caning of a chair, and this craftsman, known here only as 'Pop,' readily displays his acumen at a folk arts festival in Georgia. *At right:* The making of duck decoys is yet another studious art—some say that a good decoy is actually the product of the sum total of a man's life experience! This man shows his skill at a folk festival in Natchitoches, Louisiana. The small town seamstress *(above)* pushes her needle up from underneath, dead center of a design on her beautiful quilt, in Kentucky.

OLD-TIMER LIMITED

The urge still comes in the early spring,
  When the freight-train whistles wail;
It is then that the clicking car wheels sing
  To call me back to the rail.

As I watch the manifest roar by,
  I think of my run again,
And the long up-grade and the open sky,
  And the flags of the section men.

I hear the call of a red-hot main,
  Where the highballs fall and rise;
I hear the wind and the sleet and the rain,
  and the sound of a boomer's cries.

Yes, boys, in the spring when the oil runs free
  And the flanger's task is through,
My thoughts ride rails of memory,
  with the rest of my old-time crew.

—Earle Franklin Baker

As is explained by the plaque *above*, the town of Midway, Kentucky was actually built by a railroad. Those old tracks now form one segment of Midway's main street (*at left*); pavement and sidewalk form the other. Anyone who has grown up in Midway can tell you about the peculiar, intimate relationship that such railroad towns have with the trains that pass through them—how the *clickety clack* of the wheels on the rail sections lulls you to sleep at night, and how folks often set their schedules by the daily freight.

MY FIDDLE

My fiddle? Well, I kindo' keep her handy, don't you
    know!
Though I ain't so much inclined to tromp the strings and
    switch the bow
As I was before the timber of my elbows got so dry,
And my fingers was more limber-like and caperish and spry;
 Yit I can plonk and plunk and plink,
  And tune her up and play,
 And jest lean back and laugh and wink
  At ev'ry rainy day!

My playin's only middlin'—tunes I picked up when a boy—
The kindo'-sorto' fiddlin' that the folks calls 'corduroy;'
'The old Fat Gal,' and 'Rye-straw,' and 'My Sailor's on
    the Sea,'
Are the old cotillions I 'saw' when the choice is left to me;
 But they tell me, when I used to plink
  And plonk and plunk and play,
 My music seemed to have the kink
  O' drivin' cares away!

That's how this here old fiddle's won my heart's endurin'
    love!
From the strings acrost her middle, to the screechin' keys
    above—
From her 'apern,' over 'bridge,' and to the ribbon round her
    throat,
She's a wooin', cooin' pigeon, singin' 'Love Me' ev'ry note!
 And so I pat her neck, and plink
  Her strings with lovin' hands,
 And, listenin' close, I sometimes think
  She kindo' understands!

—Benj F Johnson, of Boone
(James Whitcomb Riley)

The folks are hopping to the strains of some prime 'down home' music at the Louisiana Heritage Fair *(above)*, in New Orleans, and over yonder in Prater's Mill, Georgia *(at right)*, one of the most charmin' fiddlers there ever was picks up on the spirit and starts sawin' away at a favorite tune.

from
TUSKEGEE

Wherefore this busy labor without rest?
Is it an idle dream to which we cling,
Here where a thousand dusky toilers sing
Unto the world their hope? 'Build we our best.
By hand and thought,' they cry, 'although unblessed.'
So the great engines throb, and anvils ring,
And so the thought is wedded to the thing;
But what shall be the end, and what the test?
Dear God, we dare not answer, we can see
Not many steps ahead, but this.

—*Leslie Pinckney Hill*

Above and below: The hard working men of the railroad. Despite modern railroad machinery, there is no replacement for the epochal 'steel drivin'' man. *At left:* Why motorists are taught to 'stop, look and listen': Having given several warning 'toots' with their airhorns, a brace of Seaboard System diesel locomotives advance their train over a grade crossing in Kingston, Georgia. *Overleaf:* A truly small town police station and city hall, on the main street of Saluda, North Carolina.

THE SAGE CRAWFISH

There was once a sage old crawfish
livin' in the swamp
and many's the child went to see him there

with darkling lantern in the twilit bayou.
So it was, so it was
the sage would speak,
glugging profundities out his beak—

and the young ones went home
transformed. Their parents
were worried, and formed

a posse to claim
that decapod of fame
and perhaps to include him in gumbo—
his wisdom he spewed,
and he afterwards stewed:
it was nothing but mumbo-jumbo!

—*Paul Thibodaux*

Well...to call them 'crawdads' in some venues will get you into a fight, but the folks at the Crawfish Festival in Breaux Bridge, Louisiana *(at left and at right)* seem purely involved in eating them and having a good time, as is the young lady *above*, who is dining on crawfish even at the Crab Festival in Lacombe! Crawfish is the name of the favorite game in Louisiana, home of Cajun/Creole cooking, which is the most distinctive regional cuisine in the United States.

REDBALL FREIGHT

The judge peered sharp at the man on trial,
   A hobo, old and gray;
He sized him up from head to toe,
   Then bade him have his say.
'Was passing through,' the 'bo spoke out,
   'On yonder streak of rust.
This cinder dick who hauled me here
   Knows naught of wanderlust.

'I had a job like yours and his
   Way back along the trail,
Arresting tramps and thieves and such
   And sending them to jail.
And then one night from in the sky
   I heard the honking geese.
They seemed to say "Come follow us
   And you will find your peace."

'A long long freight was leaving town;
   Her whistle sounded grand;
And since that night I've plied the rails
   Across our pretty land.
Now, judge, a redball's making up
   And in my heart a song
And when she leaves this town of yours
   I'd like to be along.'

'This case dismissed,' the judge then said,
   'And court's adjourned this date.
Now, hobo, you just lead the way,
   We'll nail that redball freight!'

           —H L Kelso

At left: Though one weed-ridden set of rails goes unused, the other is clean and still hosts the occasional train—and even though the passenger station *(above)* hasn't been used in years, folks in Thurmond, West Virginia still like to stop and chat awhile by the old railroad tracks.

THE GREAT

LAKES

STOP THE PRESSES

'Stop the presses!'
The editor roared
'Stop the presses!
Our readers are bored!

'News in this town
is always the same,
never a frown
and we are to blame!

'Where is the action,
the thrills, the fights?
Stories more fun
than Jenny in tights?'

The reporter sighed,
he'd heard it before,
then bolder he cried,
'There just ain't no more!'

—*R E Griffith*

Previous page: The main street of Bayfield, Wisconsin gives you a sense of what life in the Great Lakes region is like, with the blue waters of Lake Superior just on the edge of town. Though the streets may not be 'jumping,' any news is still news in Stillwater, Minnesota *(above and left)*—the kind of pristine little town many of us left behind. Where else could you buy ad space on the paper placemats in Meg's restaurant on South Main? As Ms Darien P Nordling of Stillwater's DP Advertising agency says, 'A business worth having is worth advertising; if you don't advertise it, the *Sheriff* will!' *At right:* These young swimmers are prepared to plunge into the municipal pool across from the park, down on South Main—somewhere in the great state of Illinois.

from
CONTENTMENT

Plain food is quite enough for me;
　　Three courses are as good as ten—
If Nature can subsist on three,
　　Thank Heaven for three. Amen!
I always thought cold victual nice—
　　My *choice* would be vanilla-ice.

Little I ask; my wants are few;
　　I only wish a hut of stone,
(A *very plain* brown stone will do)
　　That I may call my own—
And close at hand is such a one,
In yonder street that fronts the sun.

Thus humble let me live and die,
　　Nor long for Midas' golden touch;
If Heaven more generous gifts deny,
　　I shall not miss them *much*—
Too grateful for the blessing lent
Of simple tastes and mind content!

—Oliver Wendell Holmes

Another aspect of life in the Great Lakes region is a delicious northern European in-
fluence on such delicate items as pastry *(above)* and fine dining *(at right)*, as these are
manifested in the eateries along the main thoroughfare—with emphasis on the *fare*—
of New Glarus, Wisconsin. This is just the kind of place where the family gets into the
car and goes down town for a Saturday evening's dinner of Swedish meatballs, cab-
bage, dumplings and *strudel.*

THE HOUSE BY THE SIDE
OF THE ROAD

There are hermit souls that live withdrawn
   In the peace of their self-content;
There are souls, like stars, that dwell apart,
   In a fellowless firmament;
There are pioneer souls that blaze their paths
   Where highways never ran;
But let me live by the side of the road
   And be a friend to man.

Let me live in a house by the side of the road,
   Where the race of men go by—
The men who are good and the men who are bad,
   As good and as bad as I.
I would not sit in the scorner's seat,
   Or hurl the cynic's ban;
Let me live in a house by the side of the road
   And be a friend to man.

I see from my house by the side of the road,
   By the side of the highway of life,
The men who press with the ardor of hope,
   The men who are faint with the strife.
But I turn not away from their smiles nor their tears—
   Both parts of an infinite plan;
Let me live in my house by the side of the road
   And be a friend to man.

—Sam Walter Foss

Folks can still stop in, on a hot summer day, at the old general store in Pomona, Illinois *(left)*—a town so small it doesn't appear on most maps, but where the kindliness and courtesy just can't be beat. A friendly smile *(above)* and a cold soda pop are yours, when you ease your car in to stop a spell, just off 'Main Street.' *Overleaf:* This small Wisconsin town could be located almost anywhere in the Northern United States, with its crowded row of shops giving way abruptly to a stately little park, and then the outskirts....

Below: After a hard day on the line, or a grueling day under the schoolmaster's gaze, young and old alike retire to the Convention Grill, in Edina—Minnesota, that is—in a ritual fortification for the long night ahead. This is a covert operation that involves shakes and malts; if mother found out about it, with dinner waiting on the stove, she'd probably be mad.

AT THE DOOR

He wiped his shoes before his door,
But ere he entered he did more:
'Twas not enough to cleanse his feet
Of dirt they'd gathered in the street;
He stood and dusted off his mind
And left all trace of care behind.
'In here I will not take,' said he,
'The stains the day has brought me.

'Beyond this door shall never go
The burdens that are mine to know;
The day is done, and here I leave
The petty things that vex and grieve;
What clings to me of hate and sin
To them I will not carry in;
Only the good shall go with me
For their devoted eyes to see.

'I will not burden them with cares,
Nor track the home with grim affairs;
I will not at my table sit
With soul unclean, and mind unfit;
Beyond this door I will not take
The outward signs of inward ache;
I will not take a dreary mind
Into this house for them to find.'

He wiped his shoes before his door,
But paused to do a little more.
He dusted off the stains of strife,
The mud that's incident to life,
The blemishes of careless thought,
The traces of the fight he'd fought,
The selfish humors and the mean,
And when he entered he was clean.

—Edgar A Guest

At left: It could be Lake Woebegon, but it isn't. There is no Chatterbox Cafe in this Minnesota town, but there is a Sunnyside Road—material Garrison Keillor might easily have used in the weaving of one of his yarns. The corner drugstore is often at or near the storm center of most civic activity in such locales. Life in town can be so hectic at times, to arrive at your own front door in the evening can be downright rewarding—in fact, some folks are purely proud of it *(above)*.

THE TRIUMVIRATE

When a touch of frost
Creeps in the air
And the northwind's
Roaring bugles blare;
When the long, gray evenings
Gather down
From the hills that shadow
The walled-in town;
Oh, where is the poet
Left to sing
A song of dream
In the land of Spring?
A song of dream
That may compare
To a pipe—a book—
And an easy chair?

When the wild blasts howl
And the shadows flit
Over the wall
Where the fire is lit;
When the snow drifts deep
At the window pane;
When the dim world lies
In the pit of night,
As the gray ghosts shriek
In the mad gale's flight,
Oh where is the poet
Left to praise
The gleam and dream,
Of the summer ways?
The gleam and dream
That may compare
To a pipe—a book—
And an easy chair?

—*Grantland Rice*

At left: The old log fences and the broad main street of New Salem are covered with snow, as the heavy Illinois winter settles in. This is the perfect time for relaxing indoors.

AT THE BARBERSHOP

Ornate were the large, lettered windows
with magazines—piled here and there—
and across an expanse of hair-tufted floor
stood the barber right next to his chair.

My father, he struggled to seat me
(the barber, he simply looked glum);
they joined forces at last to defeat me—
and I finally sat on my bum.

Oh, loud was the buzz of the clippers
and close was the crop of my hair—
those electrical gadgets, those 'nippers'
had practically buzzed off my ears!

Though I meant not at all to distrust him,
still my own father's actions seemed wry—
if a bald-headed son's what he wanted,
he'd have sired one calmer than I:

For wet were my ears—all behind 'em!
and wet was the nape of my neck,
then they smothered and choked me with talcum,
and asked me to stand on the deck—

And obedient and eager to please them
(my last thought was not to defy),
I offered the sheet to the barber
and stood up and sneezed in his eye!

— *Andrew Jacobs*

Above: Nearly all of the thousand or so male residents of Mineral Point, Wisconsin have passed under this man's shears, and most of them had their first haircut at his hands. If he looks like he means business, just ask the young buck *at left* as he undergoes a boyhood rite of passage in the barber's chair.

THE EMPIRE OF NICE DREAMS

Let not seem, seem
but let every face connect its savor
to the proper cone. Let no funereal
ironies disturb our trust
in the mundane, the every-
torpid-day solidity of things
as things may be. The
only emperor's ice-cream
partakes of such as you and I.

As the best friend of lips is French vanilla,
so's the only pal of
would-be duchesses plain old 'ice'—
and let that ice be finely cut,
on sale, at half price. The only
emperor's not here my friend, nor
a connection to inscrutable
personality's loss;

but somewhere tangible as air,
right on the corner,
beyond the jewelers and the ice-cream store!

—*Andrew Jacobs*

Diamonds and ice cream, jewelers and soda jerks; polar opposites of small town life. One day you're relaxing with a cool cone as you stroll along the street—as these ladies are *(above)* in Ephraim, Wisconsin—and the next you're taking that long, serious walk to the jewelers *(at right)* to buy a set of rings that will change life entirely for you and someone that it seems you're only just getting to know....

Chestnut
Street
DIAMONDS
on main
UPSTAIRS
ABOVE STILLWATER BAKERY
95
PUSH BUTTON FOR WALK SIGNAL

82

HOME IS WHERE
THE HEART IS

Home is where the heart is,
And friendship is a guest;
A book, a fire, a handclasp,
A place where souls can rest.

Home is where the heart is,
Where children's voices ring;
A blossom at the window,
A tiny bird to sing.

Home is where the heart is,
Be it mansion on the hill,
Or cabin in the valley,
Or cottage by the rill.

Home is where the heart is,
Where friendship is a guest,
Where love and faith and gentleness
Can soothe a heart to rest.

—*Bessie Cary Dunn*

Above: Complete with trellis, sunporch and pumpkins on the lawn, this 'home, sweet home' invites you to stop awhile, and remember bygone days when Mom would ring the dinner bell, and you'd all come scurrying home. *At right:* Especially vivid is that day you and your brother surprised your old Uncle Luke as he took his ease on the back porch of his and Aunt Minnie's house way over yonder in Ontario.

THE GREAT

PLAINS

THE ROUGH LITTLE RASCAL

A smudge on his nose and a smear on his cheek
And knees that might not have been washed in
 a week;
A bump on his forehead, a scar on his lip,
A relic of many a tumble and trip;
A rough little, tough little rascal, but sweet,
Is he that each evening I'm eager to meet.

A brow that is beady with jewels of sweat;
A face that's as black as a visage can get;
A suit that at noon was a garment of white,
Now one that his mother declares is a fright:
A fun-loving, sun-loving rascal, and fine,
Is he that comes placing his black fist in mine.

A crop of brown hair that is tousled and tossed;
A waist from which two of the buttons are lost;
A smile that shines out through the dirt and the
 grime,
And eyes that are flashing delight all the time:
All these are the joys that I'm eager to meet
And look for the moment I get to my street.

—Edgar A Guest

Previous page: You can tell you're in the Great Plains when the main road through
town stretches away into the distance with nary a rise nor a fall. By the way 'Centre'
is spelled on the supermarket sign, you can tell you're in Canada—Winkler,
Manitoba, to be exact. Proof positive that the US has no monopoly on spunky little
boys: the young fellows *at left* ride their trikes like bronco busters in Thompson,
Manitoba—north of the line, as they say—while their counterparts *(above)* meditate
on a fine point of boyish balloonery 'down south' in one of those neat little Nebraska
towns.

THE HOME TOWN

Some folks leave home for money
   And some leave home for fame,
Some seek skies always sunny,
   And some depart in shame.
I care not what the reason
   Men travel east or west,
Or what the month or season—
   The home town is the best.

The home town is the glad town
   Where something real abides;
'Tis not the money-mad town
   That all its spirit hides.
Though strangers scoff and flout it
   And even jeer its name,
It has a charm about it
   No other town can claim.

The home town skies seem bluer
   Than skies that stretch away.
The home town friends seem truer
   And kinder through the day;
And whether glum or cheery
   Lighthearted or depressed,
Or struggle-fit or weary,
   I like the home town best.

—Edgar A Guest

Above: You're looking down the main street of Hartville, Wyoming, toward the hills in back of town. Everything is pretty much of a piece, yet this little scene could cause your heart to pound if you recall a childhood here.

THE OLD STORE

In the old town
     the broad street is buzzing,
Wheels are burning
     the street far and wide,
Yet the wind-flaked paint
     of the old salvage store
never fails to touch me inside.

It's a broken-down place,
     that's for certain,
but you can find there
      a rake or a hoe,
and the nutcracker grandmother
     used on the holidays—
for our dinners, so long ago!

—Andrew Jacobs

Above: Though the building's got a new brick facelift, the rather dated neon sign of this old Rexall drugstore betrays its past on a main street corner that is typical of small towns everywhere—right smack-dab in the middle of Brandon, Manitoba, where the traffic—including people, autos and baby strollers—is the heaviest in town. Over in Egbert, Wyoming *(at right)*, the old antique store there could cause a regular personal cloudburst, as a fellow picks over its relics of times past.

SONG BEFORE LEAVING

There's a freighter out of Omaha
  And on the Santa Fe
The smoky stacks are thundering
Against the Milky Way.

You know, I'd never think of leaving
If a distant whistle grieving
Wouldn't make the house I live in melt
  away—
If a rolling engine's hammer,
And the rail joint's steady stammer
Wouldn't make me see the pass at Canyon Rey.

I suppose I'd settle down
In this crowded little town
And after many years, I dare to say,
Heavy engines on the hill
While the night is dark and still,
Would leave me cold—Laredo's nice in May.

No, there are cinders in my hair,
Steam and coal smoke in the air.
Guess there isn't any more to say.
Try and understand my going
In the night—the whistles blowing—
Out under blinking stars the echoes play.
Side-rods drumming in my ears—
I've been hearing them for years.
Now they're taking me along with them
  to stay.

There's a freighter out of Omaha—
And on the Santa Fe
The smoky stacks are thundering
Against the Milky Way.

          —Patrick H Dunn

At left: As the train slows down on the outskirts of town in the Great Plains, one or two clandestine passengers might just sneak aboard, and the boys who traditionally dangle their feet off the edge of the overpass will just as traditionally see them and make a ruckus, and the engineer will also traditionally ignore the fuss, thinking -it's just his big locomotive *(above)* they're yelling for.

THE OLD HOME TOWN

The old home town
busted among its tatters
full of weeds and sudden memories
like an old car in the woods,
old Otto's corner drugstore
and long-time friends of long ago—
times of evil and of good—

arraigns us with its lamp posts, subpoenas us with sky,
hauls the wanton wayward back again without his knowing
        why.
For every tatty rosebush and every gritty street
is a family with children, and new visages you meet;

and for every broken street sign and every haggard face,
is a boy who's come to be a man, a woman full of grace—
the tree, the lawn, the civic park with robin, squirrel and mouse,
and how some folks doll up their name and stamp it
                                    on their house.

And every tree and family scene so casual imparts
the ever present threat of love
arising in our hearts—
a love to take us back again
to things we'd 'left behind'—
things we'd only stuffed down deep

that re-surface in the mind.
For every corner drugstore
and the church across from it
seems a part of long ago
but still it seems to fit

The old home town, its quiet song
will bring you to the gate
where memory proclaims aloud
    'Child, you're never really late,
    for silver hair and chances lost
    are part and parcel of the din,
    and only when the grave door's closed
    can you fail to come on in.'

—Andrew Jacobs

The folks in Rochford, South Dakota *(at right)* love their humble town much more
than they could any 'city' of 10,000 or so—yes indeed, Rochford people just love the
way their main street brings that Black Hills country beauty smack into the middle of
civilization! It also brings some wild folks and their motorbikes in from the hills, but
they usually settle down after a little while at the Moonshine Gulch Saloon *(above)*.

SILVY GAYE

Silvy one day, she dressed herself in men's array,
  With a brace of pistols by her side,
To meet her true love, to meet her true love,
  Away did ride.

She met her true love on the plain,
  And boldly bade him for to stand.
'Stand and deliver to me!' she did cry,
  'Or else this moment, or else this moment,
You shall die!'

When she had robbed him of his store,
  She said: 'Kind sir, there's one thing more—
A diamond ring I have seen you wear—
  Deliver it, deliver it,
And your life I'll spare.'

'My diamond ring is a token rare,
  My life I'll lose before I'll spare.'
She was tender-hearted, like a dove—
  She rode away, she rode away
From her true love.

It's they walked in a garden green,
  Like two young lovers oft have been seen;
He spied his watch hung by her clothes,
  Which made him blush, which made him blush,
Like any rose.

'Why blush you for so silly a thing?
  I fain would have your diamond ring.
It was I who robbed you on the plain;
  So take your gold, so take your gold, love
And watch and chain.'

Then to church they did repair,
  And like true lovers were married there.
Now James is married to Silvy Gaye—
  In joy and mirth, in joy and mirth,
They spend their days.

—Anonymous

Silvy's a sweet little gal, and since that boyfriend of hers married her, she's just blooming like a rose; actually, the folks *at left* are participants in the Regina, Saskatchewan Buffalo Days celebration. But wherever you are, the hometown 'corn' is indeed the sweetest corn. In fact, much of the Corn Palace *(above)* in downtown Mitchell, South Dakota, is rebuilt yearly with over 3000 bushels of corn.

THE SOUTHWEST

A JEWELED BUSH

Befitting its setting, an icy retreat,
A snowberry glitters in jewels of sleet;
The rain having frozen as fast as it fell,
And covered the bark with a crystalline shell.

Its wrists are encircled with bracelets of white;
Its pearlstony berries bescatter the light;
With diamond pendants its fingers are decked,
Emitting the colors that spectrums reflect.

What gems of the earth or the sea are as fair
As those that are miracled out of the air—
As those that are real, yet vanish in steam
Like fairies that flit in a beautiful dream.

—*Willis Hudspeth*

Previous page: Ancient Laguna Pueblo, west of Albuquerque, with a main street that goes back five centuries. Laguna Pueblo's streets wind up and down the hills, and the folks who live here are, sure enough, of the Laguna Pueblo people—Native Americans. *Above and at left:* Of a winter it can 'frost up' in these southwestern towns, and the most common flora can become a magically jewel-encrusted ice ornament of rare workmanship.

from
WORTER-MELON TIME

Old worter-melon time is a-comin' round again,
    And they ain't no man a-livin' any tickleder'n me,
Fer the way I hanker after worter-melons is a sin—
    Which is the why and wherefore, as you can plainly see.

Oh! it's in the sandy soil worter-melons does the best,
    And its there they'll lay and waller in the sunshine and the
        dew
Till they wear all the green streaks clean off of their breast;
    And you bet I ain't a-findin' any fault with them; are you?

It's some likes the yeller-core, and some likes the red,
    And it's some says 'the little Californy' is the best;
But the sweetest slice of all I ever wedged in my head,
    Is the old 'Edinburgh Mountain-sprout,'of the west.

I joy in my heart jest to hear that rippin' sound
    When you split one down the back and jolt the halves in
        two,
And the friends you love the best is gathered all around—
    And you says unto your sweetheart, 'Oh here's the core fer
        you!'

And I like to slice 'em up in big pieces fer 'em all,
    Especially the children, and watch their high delight
As one by one the rinds with their pink notches falls,
    And they holler fer some more, with unquenched appetite.

Boys takes to it natural, and I like to see 'em eat—
    A slice of worter-melon's like a frenchharp in their hands,
And when they 'saw' it through their mouth such music can't
        be beat—
    'Cause it's music both the spirit and the stomach under-
        stands.

Oh! it's worter-melon time is a-comin' round again,
    And they ain't no man a-livin' any tickleder'n me,
Fer the way I hanker after worter-melons is a sin—
    Which is the why and wherefore, as you can plainly see.

—Benj F Johnson, of Boone
(James Whitcomb Riley)

Above: The slices are cold and huge at the Watermelon Festival in Rush Springs, Oklahoma. The real test of a melon, though, is what happens to it in the critical hands of a bright lad; the fellow *at right* is sure to know all there is to know about water- melons! *Overleaf:* Under the shelter of an awning at a gas station, we've weathered a fierce prairie thunder storm, and now the sunshine warms the wet main street of Washington, Oklahoma.

THE FLAG GOES BY

Hats off!
Along the streets there comes
A blare of bugles, a ruffle of drums,
A flash of color beneath the sky:
    Hats off!
The flag is passing by!

Blue and crimson and white it shines
Over the steel-tipped, ordered lines.
    Hats off!
The colors before us fly;
But more than the flag is passing by.

Sea-fights and land-fights, grim and great,
Fought to make and to save the State:
Weary marches and sinking ships;
Cheers of victory on dying lips;

Days of plenty and years of peace;
March a strong land's swift increase;
Equal justice, right and law,
Stately honour and reverend awe;

Sign of a nation, great and strong
Toward her people from foreign wrong:
Pride and glory and honor—all
Live in the colors to stand or fall.

    Hats off!
Along the street there comes
A blare of bugles, a ruffle of drums;
And loyal hearts are beating high:
    Hats off!
The flag is passing by!

—Henry Holcomb Bennett

At left: The High School color guard flies Old Glory, the state flag of Oklahoma and that of their high school in a celebration of the Oklahoma Land Rush—'89er Days'— in Guthrie, Oklahoma. *Above:* The flag waves high in the bright southwestern sky—as it does in many a patriotic small town in the United States.

THE MOUNTAIN

WINNEMUCCA

Cactus, chaparral and yucca
Point the way to Winnemucca,
Where the desert nomenclature
Calls our progress back to Nature.

We are loath to leave the station
On the level desolation—
Hazy, glamorous and breezy,
Artless, chivalrous and easy.

—Willis Hudspeth

Previous page: The small community of Waterton, Alberta nestles amid the Rocky Mountain splendor of the US/Canadian Waterton International Peace Park. Interstate 80 is the main street in Winnemucca *(at left)*—where it seems like half the state of Nevada passes through on a snowy day. *Above:* Pay phones on the main drag in Wells, Nevada seem forgotten by time—or at least by inflation, which makes it easy to phone home. *Below:* The view from the western edge of Frenchman, on Nevada's Highway 50—which is 'the Main Street of America's loneliness.'

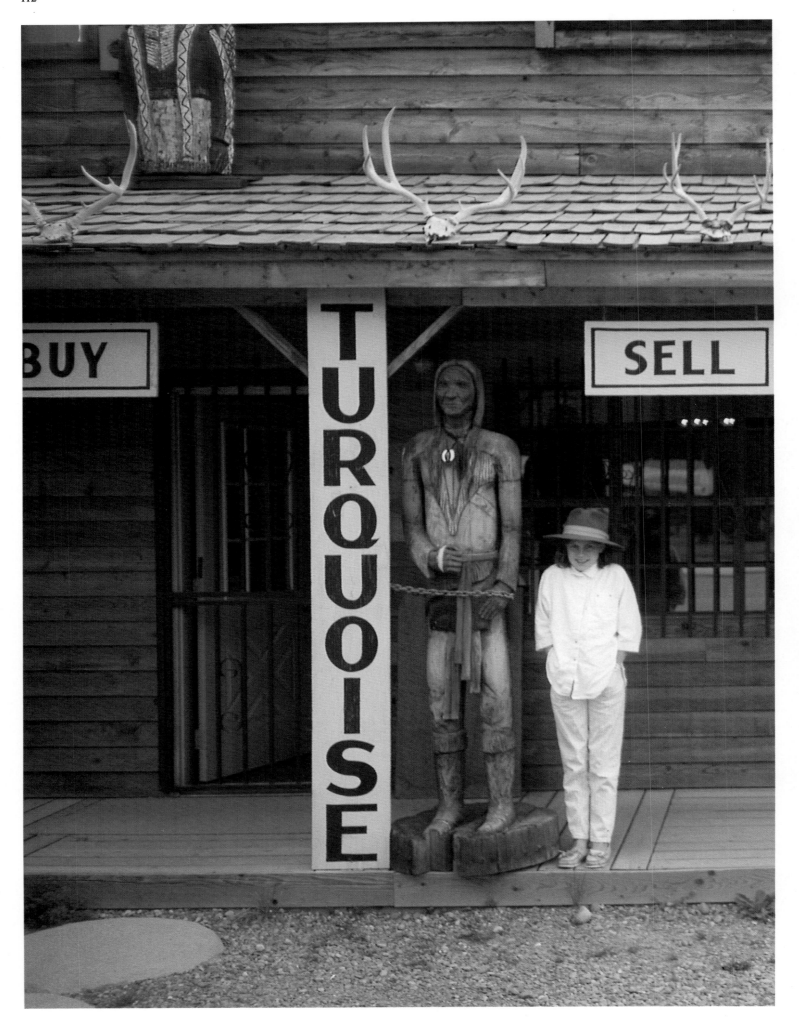

THAT OLD INDIAN

I remember the old Indian
Who posed for the statue—
The statue that stands by the front of the store.

He said he loved the town,
and more than that, mountains
Whose shadows protected
The white stucco houses
lined up in a row.

The man spoke of wonders,
how the stones of the chimneys
came down from the mountains
all rounded and polished
by the cold, pristine waters
of rampant, irascible streams.

That old Indian
he spoke of fine things
And allowed how the children
would remember his likeness—
so tall, like a pillar
in front of the store.

—Willoughby Redbluff

At right: Of course, the folks at Hungry Horse, Montana flat out invite you in by way of prominently displaying their big trading post—a general store that, by gum, has pretty near everything! But the real miracle is when you have sense enough to settle down and live in a place like Jasper, Alberta *(above)*, just to breathe in that fresh, cool Canadian Rocky Mountain air. *Overleaf:* This is Main Street for the 300 or so residents of Milltown, Montana.

TWO TAVERNS

I remember how I lay
On a bank a summer day,
Peering into weed and flower:
Watched a poppy all one hour;
Watched it till the air grew chill
In the darkness of the hill;
Till I saw a wild bee dart
Out of the cold to the poppy's heart;
Saw the petals gently spin,
And shut the little lodger in.

Then I took the quiet road
To my own secure abode.
All night long his tavern hung;
Now it rested, now it swung;
I asleep in steadfast tower,
He asleep in stirring flower;
In our hearts the same delight
In the hushes of the night
Over us both the same dear care
As we slumbered unaware.

—Edwin Markham

Sometimes on the edge of these mountain towns, you come upon a patch of flowers *(above)* so pure, pristine and dazzling that you wander, lost in thought, all the way back to your room at the inn, which could well be an establishment like the Old Saloon *(at right)*, in Dixon, Montana.

ON A SPLENDUD MATCH

He was warned against the *womern*—
She was warned against the *man*—
And ef that won't make a weddin',
Why, they's nothin' else that can!

—*Benj F Johnson, of Boone*
(James Whitcomb Riley)

Below: Great-grandpa and great-grandma would not have eloped to a place like this, located in the Sierras on the California-Nevada border (where the cities of South Lake Tahoe and Stateline share a common main street); such places did not yet exist.

from
THE WONDERFUL
ONE-HOSS SHAY

Have you heard of the wonderful one-hoss shay,
That was built in such a logical way
It ran a hundred years to a day,
And then, of a sudden, it—ah, but stay,
I'll tell you what happened without delay.

Now in building of shays, I tell you what,
There is always *somewhere* a weakest spot—
In hub, tire, felloe, in spring or thill,
In panel, or crossbar, or floor, or sill,
In screw, bolt, thoroughbrace—lurking still.

So the Deacon inquired of the village folk
Where he could find the strongest oak,
That couldn't be split nor bent nor broke—
That was for spokes and floor and sills;
The panels of white-wood, that cuts like cheese,
But lasts like iron for things like these—
Step and prop-iron, bolt and screw,
Spring, tire, axle, and linchpin too,
Steel of the finest, bright and blue—
That was the way he 'put her through.'
'There!' said the Deacon, 'now she'll do!'

Little of all we value here
Wakes on the morn of its hundredth year
Without both feeling and looking queer.

This morning *the parson* takes a drive.
Now, small boys, get out of the way!
Here comes the wonderful one-hoss shay!
'Huddup!' said the parson. Off went they.
The parson was working his Sunday text,
Had got to *fifthly,* and stopped perplexed
At what the—Moses—was coming next.
All at once the horse stood still.
Close by the meet'n-house on the hill.
First a shiver, and then a thrill,
Then something decidedly like a spill—

What do you think the parson found,
When he got up and stared around?
The poor old shay in a heap or mound,

As if it had been to the the mill and ground!
You see, of course, if you're not a dunce,
How it went to pieces all at once—
All at once, and nothing first—
Just as bubbles do when they burst.

End of the wonderful one-hoss shay.
Logic is logic. That's all I say.

—*Oliver Wendell Holmes*

At right: The kids seem a little unsure, Mom is busy trying to get Dobbin out of his balk, and Dad's taking the picture of this 'one-hoss shay' family outing in a pretty, small town Alberta setting.

from
LIVING

I wouldn't call it living to be always seeking gold,
To bank all the present gladness for the days when
    I'll be old.
I wouldn't call it living to spend all my strength for
    fame,
And forego the many pleasures which today are mine
    to claim.
I wouldn't for the splendor of the world set out to
    roam,
And forsake my laughing children and the peace I
    know at home.

Oh, the thing that I call living isn't gold or fame at
    all!
It's fellowship and sunshine, and it's roses by the
    wall.
It's evenings glad with music and a hearth-fire that's
    ablaze.
And the joys which come to mortals in a thousand
    different ways.
It is laughter and contentment and the struggle for a
    goal;
It is everything that's needful in the shaping of a soul.

—Edgar A Guest

Above: The boys stroll beside Pop, who is just beginning to sing a cowboy song. Altogether, these three couldn't give a hoot for the hustle and bustle, as they mosey along the sidewalk in Helena, Montana. *At left:* Eddie's Cafe, on the main street of Apgar, in beautiful Glacier National Park, Montana. Apgar's handful of citizens are fanatically devoted to the study of the town's history—which predates, but is intimately entwined with, that of the Park. For instance, Eddie Brewster was the son of Horace Brewster, the first park ranger in Glacier National Park, and was raised in the North Fork area of the park. After working as a ranger himself, Eddie and his wife bought Bill Mackin's old grocery store back in 1946, and added the restaurant that has evolved into the Eddie's Cafe of today.

from
THE SCHOOLHOUSE WINDOWS

Hope builded herself a palace
  At the heart of the oak-roofed town,
And out of its airy windows
  Her happy eyes looked down:

Full many a changing face has she
  For the changing earth below,
And to each the magical windows
  A different picture show.

So each of the childish faces,
  That looks out into the air,
Through an image of itself must see
  That colors all things there;

Our lives are but what we see them;
  Bright, if the eye-beams are—
Not what shines in, but what shines out,
  Makes every world a star.

So when at the schoolhouse windows
  They stand, the guileless wise,
I peer o'er the clustered shoulders,
  And see with their own bright eyes.

—*Edward Rowland Sill*

Previous page: The folks have all come out for Sunday services at the First Baptist Church in the Missoula, Montana of more than 30 years ago. Wherever you are in the mountains, the schoolhouse *(at right)* is sure to be a big item in any town; and schooling itself often extends beyond those 'schoolhouse windows,' as is demonstrated by the Junior Girl Scout *above*, who shares a bit of 'learning' with her little sister.

AFEARED OF A GAL

Oh, darn it all! Afeared of her,
  And such a mite of a gal;
Why, two of her size rolled into one
  Won't ditto sister Sal!
Her voice is sweet as the whippoorwill's,
  And the sunshine's in her hair;
But I'd rather face a redskin's knife,
  Or the grip of a grizzly bear.
Yet Sal says, 'Why, she's such a dear,
  She's just the one for you.'
Oh, darn it all! Afeared of a gal,
  And me just six feet two!

Though she ain't any size, while I'm
  Considerable tall,
I'm nowhere when she speaks to me,
  She makes me feel so small.
My face grows red, my tongue gets hitched;
  The cussed thing won't go;
It riles me, 'cause it makes her think
  I'm most tarnation slow.
And though folks say she's sweet on me,
  I guess it can't be true.
Oh, darn it all! Afeared of a gal,
  And me just six feet two!

—Anonymous

Above: The VFW post in Hungry Horse, Montana. VFW posts often sponsor dances for the youth of a community. As a result of even such a well-intended function as that, you could wind up in the awful situation of the young fellow *at right*—with that girl who's been bothering you ever since you met at the dance on one side and *your older sister* on the other! This tragic scene took place in the state capital of Montana, where the main street is called Last Chance Gulch.

from
THE PREACHER

In the church of the wilderness Edwards wrought,
Shaping his creed at the forge of thought;
And with Thor's own hammer welded and bent
The iron links of his argument,
Which strove to grasp in its mighty span
The purpose of God and the fate of man!
Yet faithful still, in his daily round
To the weak, and the poor, and sin-sick found
The schoolman's lore and the casuist's art
Drew warmth and life from his fervent heart.
Had he not seen in the solitudes
Of his deep and dark Northampton woods
A vision of love about him fall?

Lo! by the Merrimac Whitefield stands
In the temple that never was made by hands—
Curtains of azure, and crystal wall,
And dome of the sunshine over all—
A homeless pilgrim, with dubious name
Blown about on the winds of fame;
Now as an angel of blessing classed,
And now as a mad enthusiast.
Called in his youth to sound and gauge
The moral lapse of his race and age,
And, sharp as truth, the contrast draw
Of human frailty and perfect law;
Possessed by the one dread thought that lent
Its goad to his fiery temperament,
Up and down the world he went,
A John the Baptist crying, Repent!

Under the church of Federal Street,
Under the tread of its Sabbath feet,
Walled about by its basement stones,
Lie the marvellous preacher's bones.
No saintly honors to them are shown,
No sign nor miracle have they known;
But he who passes the ancient church
Stops in the shade of its belfry-porch,
And ponders the wonderful life of him
Who lies at rest in that charnel dim.

Still, as the gem of its civic crown,
Precious beyond the world's renown,
His memory hallows the ancient town!

—John Greenleaf Whittier

Previous page: One aspect of a Canadian main street wherever you go is the presence—or absence—of the Mounties. Shown here is the Royal Canadian Mounted Police station at Waterton, Alberta. In wilderness, Mounties do use horses, and in the Far North, even dog sleds, but in town—just as with any town constable—the vehicle of choice is the automobile. *At left:* The Boise Valley Baptist Church. The name 'Boise' is common to a number of features—including the state capital—within the 'spud state,' Idaho. This simple wooden white-washed church is typical for a Baptist church in its spareness, which spareness also extends to the typical Baptist service, and is reflected in the straightforward Baptist approach to life.

MY MOTHER'S HANDS

Such beautiful, beautiful hands!
  They're neither white nor small;
And you, I know, would scarcely think
  That they were fair at all—

Such beautiful, beautiful hands!
  Though heart were weary and sad,
These patient hands kept toiling on,
  That the children might be glad;
I always weep, as looking back
  To childhood's distant day,
I think how those hands rested not,
  When mine were at their play.

Such beautiful, beautiful hands!
  They're growing feeble now,
For time and pain have left their mark
  On hands, and heart, and brow—

But oh, beyond this shadow land,
  Where all is bright and fair,
I know full well these dear old hands
  Will palms of victory bear!

—Anonymous

Above: Near parade's end, this Native American mother obviously has her hands full at a Frontier Days celebration on Missoula, Montana's main street. Soon enough, she and her kids will join Poppa, and they will retire to their home town of Moiese *(at right)*, which is not quite big enough to have its own Frontier Days celebration.

TONY'S YARD

There is no more inspiring yard
Than Tony's on the boulevard,
Where, in the middle of the green,
A sprinkler like the Hippocrene
Is mixing with its iris jets
The purple of the violets.

A garden hose is curved across
The close-cut rye grass, edged with moss,
Two fragile oleander shrubs
Are blossoming from painted tubs;
A half a dozen olives wave
Their tranquil branchlets by the pave.

A stuffed flamingo perches near
The twisted grapevines in the rear;
In gaudy gingham Tony's spouse
Is shifting round the little house,
Uprooting, ere the day is gone,
The fecund darnel from the lawn.

—*Willis Hudspeth*

And some people have all the luck, living in luxury on the boulevard *(above)* in the university town of Missoula, Montana. *At left:* This Stetsoned mistress of the house smiles to see that all is well-ordered in her garden at Three Forks, Montana. *Overleaf:* Sometimes, when you're driving for hours and you come upon a place like Dayton it seems like a little bit of mercy in the wilderness reaches of Wyoming—to stop a bit and rest by the main artery of town, I mean.

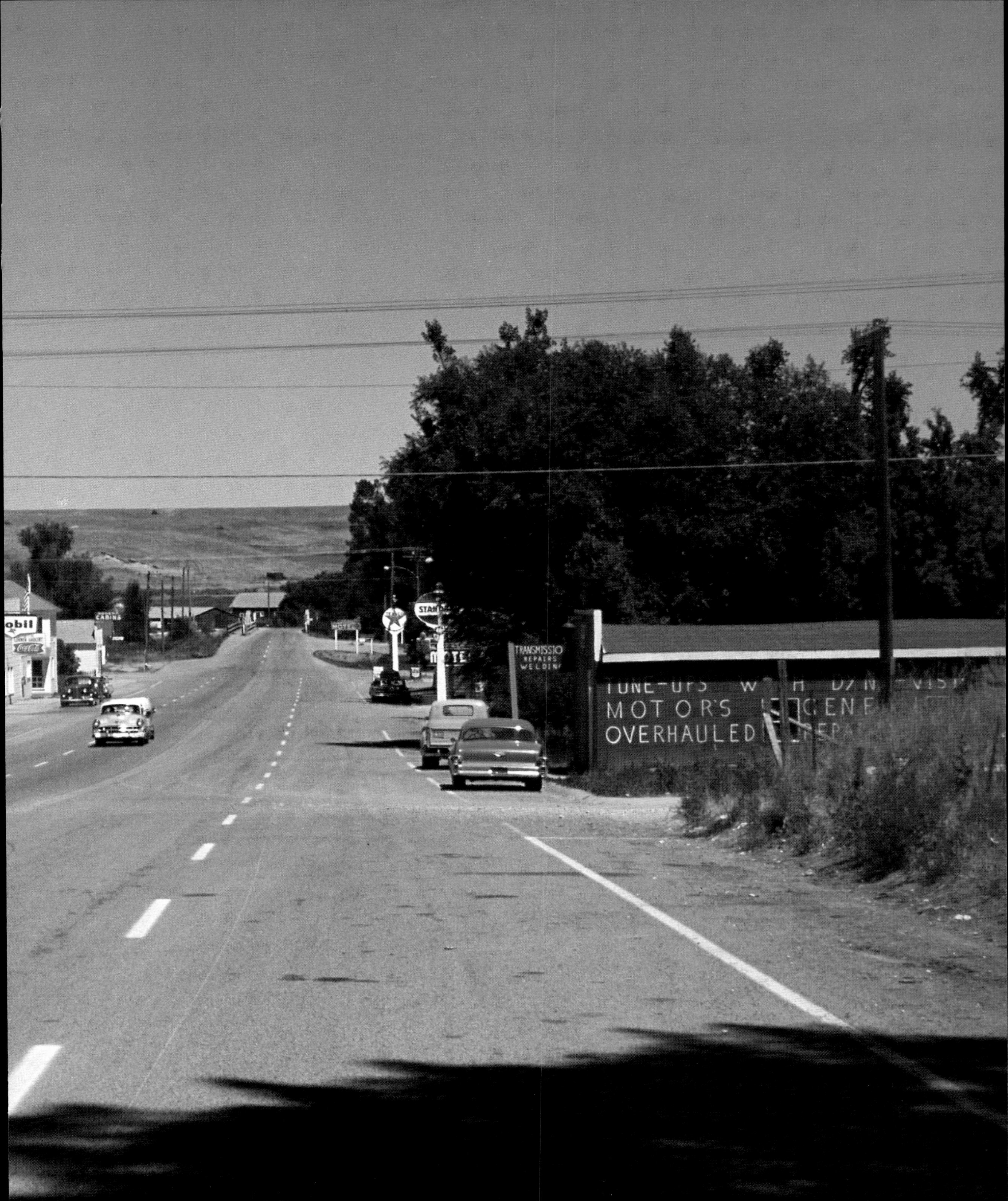
TRANSMISSIO
REPAIRS
WELDING
TUNE-UPS
MOTOR'S
OVERHAULED

WINTER

The air is keen, the sky is clear,
   The winds have gone in whispers down;
And gleaming in the atmosphere,
   A jewel, lies the lighted town,

The winter's mantle stretches white
   Upon the roofs and streets below;
All hushed the noises of the night,
   Against the bosom of the snow.

The moon from her blue dwelling-place
   Smiles over all, so pale, so fair,
It seems the Earth's wan, winter face
   Reflected in a mirror there.

Far off the lonely trees uplift
   Their naked branches, like the spars
Of some deserted ship adrift
   Under a canopy of stars.

It is the darkened world that rides
   The sea of space, forever drawn
By secret winds and mighty tides
   Unto the harbor of the Dawn.

—Frank D Sherman

At left: The first snowfall of the season is very special, with the almost inaudible hiss of the snow laying down in a soft, thick twilit blanket—but just wait until it really gets going; the magic could be said to *snowball.*

THE FAR NORTH

ALASKAN PIPELINE

Quonset hut, teepee—
it's all the same to me;
but since I joined this
roughneck crew,
nothing but the windy North will do.

For months we drove the pipleline,
    crossed the rough Alaskan waste.
One frozen night I broke my foot
and took the sick time that I faced.
On the coast, the Russian monks
    live in monasteries bare,
and never had I felt so blessed
    to spend that wounded winter
by their lair—one night I thought
    I saw an angel there.

And again, I'm on the pipeline,
    and I work from town to town,
and when we come to Prospect Creek
    I'll lay my Stillson down—yes, I'll
lay that old wrench down. Believe
    I'll pray to old Saint Herman
and lay that big wrench down.

—Andrew Jacobs

Previous page: One of the prominent buildings in Whitehorse, Yukon Territory is actually a boat! And well, it's not so strange to honor your most important thoroughfare in such a fitting way, for the *real* main street of not only Whitehorse, but of most the Yukon, is the Yukon River. Whitehorse itself is the prominent town of Yukon Territory, being its capital, and having a population of 13,311. *At left* is the village of Prospect Creek, which grew up as a way station of the Alyeska Pipeline operation. The Alyeska Pipeline is to Alaska—as is the Yukon River to Yukon Territory—a main street in itself, with many towns having grown up along its length. Both the pipeline and the river perform functions which are associated with those of the main street in any town. The river is an avenue by which contact is made with other parts of the Yukon, goods and supplies are traded, and people come and go. The pipeline connects Alaska's bustling hubs of human activity with its fringes—like the river, tending to form a thoroughfare along which civilization plays out its daily routine. *Above* is a closeup of some of Prospect Creek's inhabitants hard at work. Like the inhabitants of any classical small American town, these fellows know that the main street of where they live is also their livelihood.

from
FOLKS

We was speakin' of folks, jes' common folks,
   An' we come to this conclusion,
That wherever they be, on land or sea,
   They warm to a home allusion;
That under the skin an' under the hide
   There's a spark that starts a-glowin'
Whenever they look at a scene or book
   That something of home is showin.'

Now folks is folks on their different way,
   With their different griefs an' pleasures,
But the home they knew, when their years were few,
   Is the dearest of all their treasures.
Time may robe 'em in sackcloth coarse
   Or garb 'em in gorgeous splendor,
But whatever their lot, they keep one spot
   Down deep that is sweet an' tender.

We was speakin' of folks, jes' common folks,
   An' we come to this conclusion,
That one an' all, be they great or small,
   Will warm to a home allusion;
That under the skin an' the beaten hide
   They're kin in a real affection
For the joys they knew, when their years were few,
   An' the home of their recollection.

—Edgar A Guest

Of course in other parts of the Far North, folks know that life just simply does not consist solely of busting one's knuckles with a pipe wrench in the freezing cold—in fact it makes a lot more sense to have a village blanket toss *(above)*, or to have a night out on the tundra with the other ladies—which these grandmothers *at right* are preparing to do, as they set out down Main Street in Kotzebue, Alaska. *Overleaf:* The main street of Skagway, Alaska, with the Coast Mountains rising up at the edge of town.

from
THE GRAMAPHONE
AT FOND-DU-LAC

Now Eddie Malone got a swell grammyfone to
    draw all the trade to his store;
An' sez he: 'Come along for a season of song, which
    the like ye had niver before.'
Then Dogrib, an' Slave, an' Yellowknife brave, an' Cree
    in his dinky canoe,
Confluated near, to see an' to hear Ed's grammyfone
    make its dayboo.

Then Ed turned the crank, an' there on the bank they
    squatted like bumps on a log.
For acres around there wasn't a sound, not even the
    howl of a dog.
When out of the horn there sudden was born such a
    marvellous elegant tone;
An' then like a spell on that audience fell the voice
    of its first grammyfone.

Then sudden an' clear there rang on my ear a song
    mighty simple an' old;
Heart-hungry an' high it thrilled to the sky, all about
    'silver threads in the gold.'
'Twas tender to tears, an' it brung back the years, the
    mem'ries that hallow an' yearn;
'Twas home-love an' joy, 'twas the thought of my boy
    . . . an' right there I vowed I'd return.

Big Four-finger Jack was right at my back, an' I saw
    with a kind o' surprise,
He gazed at the lake with a heartful of ache, an' the
    tears irrigated his eyes.
An' sez he: 'Cuss me, pard! but that there hits me
    hard; I've a mother does nuthin' but wait.
She's turned eighty-three, an' she's only got me, an'
    I'm scared it'll soon be too late.'

On Fond-du-lac's shore I'm hearin' once more that blessed
    old grammyfone play.
The summer's all gone, an' I'm still livin' on in the same
    old haphazardous way.
Oh, I cut the booze, an' with muscles an' thews I
    corralled all the coin to go back;
But it wasn't to be: he'd a mother, you see, so I—
    slipped it to Four-finger Jack.

—*Robert Service*

At right: These two young ladies seem thrilled to hear the gramaphone, or is it just the cold—at Inuvik, in Canada's Northwest Territories. *Above:* This clever fellow, who enacts Robert Service at the historic Robert Service Cabin in Dawson City, Yukon Territory, looks more like 'Eddy Malone.'

COASTING

The bundled youngsters climb the hill and tow
   The sled to the summit of the street
   To fill it single-fashion and repeat
The swift descension on the beaten snow.
A rugged rider with his cheeks aglow
   Has grasped the handles at the foremost seat
   Some others place the stirrups on their feet;
The last one, mounting, shoves them off to go.

A whiskered Airedale lifts his icy ears
   To enter in the spirit of the dash;
He barks applause, in answer to the cheers,
   And leaps to pass the gliders in a flash,
But turns a wagless bobtail when he hears
   The jeering at a running dog so rash.

               —*Willis Hudspeth*

Above: These two young lads are ready to breach the fields of
snow on the fringe of their home town, which is Yellowknife,
in Canada's Northwest Territories.

from
SEPPALA DRIVES TO WIN!

There's a race on the Trail into Candle
With a Nome Sweepstakes team in the game—
Hear the rhythm and beat of the fast flying feet
Of the dogs that have earned them a name!
But this contest is not for a record,
Neither cup nor a purse is the goal;
For Seppala, intent, on one mission is bent—
Of racing with Death for a Soul.

For at Dime there was crushed, in a moment,
Bobby Brown, well beloved far and wide;
Whose life ebbing fast strikes the driver aghast,
As he faces his harrowing ride.

There's the broken and pain-tortured body
Lying heavy on Stevenson's lap;
There are unuttered fears, and his friend's bitter tears,
As they fasten each buckle and strap.
Then, the swift-spoken word to the leader,
While as swiftly he answers the same:
'There's a race to be run, and a stake to be won—
Come, Togo, live up to your name.'

They are dashing o'er limitless tundra
Over Depths where the ice menace lies;
And the glare of the sun, on that nerve-racking run,
Is a flame to their half-blinded eyes.

There's the sting and the rage of the blizzards,
As the Arctic unleashes its gale;
There's ice hanging off of their gizzards,
There's Death riding hard on their Trail,
Man's pluck, and the strength of a dog-team—
'On Togo! We trust to your pace'
There's the flash of a light—then there's Candle in sight
And Seppala beats Death in the Race!

—*Esther Birdsall Darling*

Though they are not necessarily 'big' dogs, sled dogs have to be—and are—strong,
and have to possess unusual canine endurance and intelligence; the Siberian husky
was bred for just those qualities. *Above:* This team won first prize at the Trapper's
Festival held at The Pas, in Northern Manitoba. *At right:* Mush you huskies! Seppala's
sled team might have looked a bit like this one, which is blasting down the snowpack
on the main street of Whitehorse, in Canada's Yukon Territory.

THE PACIFIC

COAST

from
OLD FRIENDS

New friends may be fond of you for what
    you are like now;
They've only known you rich, perhaps, an' only
    seen you glow;
You can't tell what's attracted them; your
    station may appeal;
Perhaps they smile on you because you're doin'
    something real;
But old friends who have seen you fail, an' also
    seen you win,
Who've loved you either up or down, stuck
    to you, thick or thin,
Who knew you as a budding youth, an' watched
    you start to climb,
Through weal an' woe, still friends of yours
    an' constant all the time,
When trouble comes an' things go wrong, I
    don't care what you say,
They are the friends you'll turn to, for you
    want the old friends' way.

—*Edgar A Guest*

Previous page: From one coast to another, it may be a long time between fishing boats like these—but if you live on Bay Boulevard, the main street of Newport, Oregon, this is what the view 'at the foot of town' looks like. Of course, some people see fishing in a less commercial light, like the friendly folks *above*, who just practically caught these salmon from their own front steps in Campbell River, British Columbia—just off the Georgia Strait. *At right:* Three friendly chefs at the Harbor Days festival in Gig Harbor, Washington. Fella on the left is the manager of the operation, fella in the middle is the nervous genius and the guy on the right knows good eatin', so come dig in!

A CIRCUS

The greatest show on earth will soon commence
    A burnished band is playing fast and loud;
    Enlarging to the street, a motley crowd
Is pushing for admission to the tents.
Anxiety is growing with suspense;
    The toiler with his children, sweaty-browed,
    The rich, the lame, the aged and the proud
Are driving in a justified offense.

Assembled is the trick menagerie
    From ev'ry foreign sea and jungled shore;
A ticket-seller spiels persuasively
    Of freaks and monsters pictured round the door.
The clowns are there, the racing gaiety,
    And acrobats that we have seen before.

—Willis Hudspeth

Above: Some circuses stay on the ground, some take to the air—this clown is about to fly this excited girl to the heights of the big top at the Harbor Days festival in Gig Harbor, Washington. *At right:* In Ellensburg, in the Evergreen State, the whole town turns out for the Rodeo Parade. Here a clown greets a young spectator. Clowns are often the bravest performers in a rodeo, distracting with their own bodies huge bulls—which would otherwise trample their 'thrown' riders.

THE VILLAGE BLACKSMITH

Under a spreading chestnut tree
  The village smithy stands;
The smith, a mighty man is he,
  With large and sinewy hands;
And the muscles of his brawny arms
  Are strong as iron bands.

His hair is crisp, and black, and long;
  His face is like the tan;
His brow is wet with honest sweat;
  He earns whate'er he can,
And looks the whole world in the face,
  For he owes not any man.

Week in, week out, from morn till night,
  You can hear his bellows blow;
You can hear him swing his heavy sledge,
  With measured beat and slow,
Like a sexton ringing the village bell
  When the evening sun is low.

And children coming home from school
  Look in at the open door;
They love to see the flaming forge,
  And hear the bellows roar,
And catch the burning sparks that fly
  Like chaff from a threshing-floor.

He goes on Sunday to the church,
  And sits among his boys;
He hears the parson pray and preach,
  He hears his daughter's voice,
Singing in the village choir,
  And it makes his heart rejoice.

It sounds to him like her mother's voice,
  Singing in Paradise!
He needs must think of her once more,
  How in the grave she lies;
And with his hard, rough hand he wipes
  A tear out of his eyes.

Toiling—rejoicing—sorrowing—
  Onward through life he goes:
Each morning sees some task begin,
  Each evening sees it close;
Something attempted—something done,
  Has earned a night's repose.

Thanks, thanks to thee, my worthy friend,
  For the lesson thou has taught!
Thus at the flaming forge of Life
  Our fortunes must be wrought,
Thus on its sounding anvil shaped
  Each burning deed and thought.

—Henry Wadsworth Longfellow

At right: In tiny (population: 18), yet historic, Harmony, California, the smithy still wears its sign—if you were to knock at the door here, would a booming, friendly voice invite you in? Or has the smith gone on to join his wife, and does their daughter, now a mother, chance to hear her son's manly voice in the church choir—and does his voice evoke her tears?

from
THE FLOWER I GREW

In pensive mood,
I walked along the garden path one day,
And there beside the wall where shines the sun
I cleared a little place and dug a hole,
And planted there a seed, only one.

In careless mood,
I walked along the path again one day,
And on the stem two tiny leaves I found.
My heart leaped up! A miracle I saw,
A growing thing made this a hallowed ground.

In happy mood,
I went to see my flower every day,
And dug and sprayed and watered it with care.
My heart rejoiced when each new leaf appeared,
My friends came out to see, my joy to share.

In joyous mood,
I watched each day a tiny bud unfold
And slowly opened leaves of rarest shade,
A velvet pink no artist's brush could tint;
It was my own, its beauty I had made.

(O changing mood!)
A full-blown bloom I plucked one day with care
And placed it in a vase where I could see.
I think I never saw a flower so rare
As one I grew and watched from day to day!

—Julia S Anderson

The towns on Vancouver Island, British Columbia, are renowned for their gardens *(at left)* and such magnificent excuses for floral displays as the 'Second Castle' *(above)*, in Victoria—a large but very stately town, indeed. Vancouver Island is home to a number of towns, and a very large number of gardens.

from
THE FALLING OF THE PINE

Come all young men that's wanted,
And you that's not undaunted,
Repair and go to shanty life
   Before your youth declines,
Spectators they will ponder—
They will look at us and wonder—
As our noise succeeds to thunder,
   At the falling of the pine.

When daylight is a-breaking,
From our slumbers we're awakened;
When our breakfast we have taken,
   Our axes we go grind;

And to the woods advance,
Where our axes clear do glance,
And like brothers we'll commence
   To fall the stately pine.

The woods it is our elation,
Likewise our occupation;
Every man at his station!
   There's some to score and line,
With the right foot at the block;
We will chip it every knock—
The deer and wolves we'll shock,
   At the falling of the pine.

Now I hope to be excused—
Hope not to be ill-used—
Since my feeble pen refused
   To write another line.
That in holy Paradise
We may unite our voice,
And like brothers we'll rejoice,
   Like the days we falled the pine.

—*Henry A Burton*

Whereas enormous Paul Bunyan would have just stuffed such toothpicks in his pockets, modern loggers haul massive logs with equally massive diesel trucks, such as this rig *(at left)*, which is on parade at the Logger's Jubilee, in Morton, Washington. Morton townfolk *(above)* turn out each year to test their abilities at such grueling contests as sawing a three-foot thick log through in under a minute. An old foreman helps out here by cooling the sizzling sawblade with water.

from
THE HOUSE AND THE HEART

Every house with its garret,
Lumbered with rubbish and relics—
Spinning-wheels leaning in corners,
Chests under spider-webbed rafters,
Brittle and yellow old letters,
Grandfather's things and grandmother's.
There overhead, at the midnight,
Noises of creaking and stepping
Startle the hush of the chambers—
Ghosts on their tiptoes repassing.

Every house with its garden;
Some little plot—a half-acre,
Or a mere strip by the windows,
Flowerbeds and narrow box-borders,
Something spicily fragrant,
Something azure and golden.
There the small feet of the sparrow
Star the fresh mould round the roses;
And, in the shadowy moonlight,
Wonderful secrets are whispered.

Every heart with its garret,
Cumbered with relics and rubbish—
Wheels that are silent forever,
Leaves that are faded and broken,
Foolish old wishes and fancies,
Cobwebs of doubt and suspicion—
Useless, unbeautiful, growing
Year by year thicker and faster:
Naught but a fire or a moving
Ever can clear it, or clean it.

Every heart with its garden;
Some little corner kept sacred,
Fragrant and pleasant with blossoms;
There the forget-me-nots cluster,
And pure love-violets, hidden,
Guessed but by sweetness all round them;
Some little strip in the sunshine,
Cheery and warm, for above it
Rest the deep, beautiful heavens,
Blue, and beyond and forever.

—Edward Rowland Sill

In the attics and crawl spaces hidden under the shingles of many small town rooftops, many memories are stored; the perambulator *(at right)* which Grandma wheeled old Dad in while she walked beside Grandpa in the Election Day parade has only just recently been recovered by 'the kids,' who are now themselves known as 'Mom and Dad.' Dad brought his bride home here, many years ago—the place was freshly repainted then, and it was obvious that even after they died, Grandma and Grandpa would live on in the old house, for the same old caring and warmth was reborn in the younger generation. And this house, situated on the corner of a northern California main street, will be remade over again for the children's children.

THE DOORSTEP

The conference-meeting through at last,
  We boys around the vestry waited
To see the girls come tripping past
  Like snow-birds willing to be mated.

Not braver he who leaps the wall
  By level musket flashes litten,
Than I, that stepped before them all
  Who longed to see me get the mitten.

But no, she blushed and took my arm!
  We let the old folks have the highway,
And started toward the Maple Lane
  Along a kind of lovers' byway.

I can't remember what we said,
  'Twas nothing worth a song or story;
Yet that rude path by which we sped
  Seemed all transformed and in a glory.

To have her with me there alone—
  'Twas love and fear and triumph blended.
At last we reached the foot-worn stone
  Where that delicious journey ended.

The old folks, too, were almost home;
  Her dimpled hand the latches fingered,
We heard the voices nearer come,
  Yet on the doorstep still we lingered.

My lips till then had only known
  The kiss of mother and of sister,
But somehow, full upon her own
  Sweet mouth—I kissed her!

—*E C Stedman*

At left: Built as an opera house, this edifice at the corner of Eighth and Albany streets in Elgin, Oregon became 'City Hall' when Elgin's citizenry turned their backs on theater in favor of the nitty-gritty realities of municipal life. However, theater began once again to encroach on reality and now the place is being restored to as near its original condition as is possible. Most of City Hall has moved out of the building, though the police and the courts are still there, and it may be hard to get them to move.

For instance, it's been rumored that on days when business is slow, the chief can be found munching popcorn in the theater, his eyes glued to yet another viewing of *Dirty Harry*. The only place of its kind in the country, it holds a well-deserved spot on the national register of historic places. After a long movie following a hard day at court, it could be mighty nice to walk yourself—or someone you like—to a fine front door like this one *(above)*, down the street.

UPHILL

Does the road wind uphill all the way?
  Yes, to the very end.
Will the day's journey take the whole long day?
  From morn to night, my friend.

But is there for the night a resting place?
  A roof for when the slow, dark hours begin.
May not the darkness hide it from my face?
  You cannot miss that inn.

Shall I meet other wayfarers at night?
  Those who have gone before.
Then must I know, or call when just in sight?
  They will not keep you standing at that door.

Shall I find comfort, travel sore and weak?
  Of labour you shall find the sum.
Will there be beds for me and all who seek?
  Yea, beds for all who come.

—Christina G Rossetti

Previous page: Flapjacks are in abundance on 'Main Street,' at a 'pancake feed' during the annual rodeo parade in Ellensburg, Washington. California's rising, falling and winding State Highway 1 forms a main street as it passes through Olema *(at left)*. This weathered but inviting old country house *(above)* in Bodega, California fronts a similar civic thoroughfare, and is the apparent center of a healthy, if informal, commercial enterprise.

OUR DUTY TO OUR FLAG

Less hate and greed
Is what we need
And more of service true;
More men to love
The flag above
And keep it first in view.

Less boast and brag
About the flag,
More faith in what it means;
More heads erect,
More self-respect,
Less talk of war machines.

The time to fight
To keep it bright
Is not along the way,
Nor 'cross the foam,
But here at home
Within ourselves—today.

—*Edgar A Guest*

Above: In Mokelumne Hill, California, as in small towns across the United States, the volunteer fire company, which as an institution is nearly as symbolic as Old Glory is of independence and community duty, figures prominently in flag-waving Fourth of July celebrations. *At right:* America's complex heritage is doubly evident in this view of a reproduction Revolutionary War-era flag flying above one of 'Detroit's finest'—which itself had rattled and rumbled down Volcano, California's tiny main street in an earlier, purer time.

from
ERASMUS WILSON

'Ras Wilson, I respect you, 'cause
You're common, like you allus was
Afore you went to town and s'prised
The world by gettin' 'reckonized,'
And yet preservin,' as I say,
Your common hoss-sense ev'ryway!
And when that name o'yourn occurs
On hand-bills or in newspapers,
Or letters writ by friends that ask
About you, same as in the past,
And neighbors and relations allow
You're out of' the tall timber now!
'Ras Wilson! Say! Hold up! and shake
A paw, fer old acquaintance sake!

Dad-burn ye! Like to jest haul back
A' old flat-hander, jest che-whack!
And take you 'twixt the shoulders, say,
Sometime you're lookin' t'other way!
And talk and chaw! Talk o' the birds
We've knocked with crossbows. Afterwards
Drop, maybe, into some dispute
'Bout 'pomgrannies,' er calamus root—
And how they growed, and whare—on tree
Or vine? Who's best boy-memory!
And wasn't it gingsang, instead
O' Calmus-root, growed like you said?

Dag-gone it, Ras! They hain't no friend,
It 'pears-like, left to comprehend
Such things as these but you, and see
How dratted sweet they are to me!
But you, 'at's loved 'em allus, and
Kin sort 'em out and understand
'Em, same as the fine books you've read,
And all fine thoughts you've writ, or said,
Or worked out, through long nights o'rain,
And doubts and fears, and hopes, again,
As bright as morning when she broke—
You know a teardrop from a joke!
    And so, 'Ras Wilson, stop and shake
    A paw, fer old acquaintance sake!

—*Benj F Johnson, of Boone*
(James Whitcomb Riley)

At left: Two long-time pals—the one looking a little worse for the wear—discuss the finer points of today's thoroughbreds in a bit of sidewalk camaraderie, at a Main Street news stand in 'Beautiful' British Columbia.

CALIFORNIA WINTER

This is not winter: where is the crisp air,
And snow upon the roof, and frozen ponds,
And the star-fire that tips the icicle?

Here blooms the late rose, pale and odorless;
And the vague fragrance in the garden walks
Is but a doubtful dream of mignonette.
In some smooth spot, under a sleeping oak
That has not dreamed of such a thing as spring,
The ground has stolen a kiss from the cool sun
And thrilled a little, and the tender grass
Has sprung untimely, for these great bright days,
Staring upon it, will not let it live.
The sky is blue, and 'tis a goodly time,
And the round, barren hillsides tempt the feet;
But'tis not winter: such as seems to man
What June is to the roses, sending floods
Of life and color through the tingling veins.

Far is the old home, where, even this night,
Roars the great chimney with its glorious fire,
And old friends look into each other's eyes
Quietly, for each knows the other's trust.

Heaven is not far away such winter night:
The big white stars are sparkling in the east,
And glitter in the gaze of solemn eyes;
For many things have faded with the flowers,
And many things their resurrection wait;
Earth like a sepulchre is sealed with frost,
And Morn and Even beside the silent door
Sit watching, and their soft and folded wings
Are white with feathery snow.

Yet even here
We are not quite forgotten by the Hours,
Could human eyes but see the beautiful
Save through the glamour of a memory.
Soon comes the strong south wind, and shouts aloud
Its jubilant anthem. Soon the singing rain
Comes from warm seas, and its skyey tent
Enwraps the drowsy world. And when, some night,
Its flowing folds invisibly withdraw,
Lo, the new life in all created things!
The azure mountains and the ocean gates
Against the lovely sky stand clean and clear
As a new purpose in the wiser soul.

—Edward Roland Sill

Below: Winter in Mendocino, California is just plain not as dramatic—nor as severe—as winter in other locales. Still, some people claim that the *sunlight* changes at this time of year....

LET ME GROW LOVELY

Let me grow lovely, growing old—
   So many fine things to do;
Laces, and ivory, and gold,
   And silks need not be new.

And there is healing in old trees,
   Old streets a glamour hold;
Why may not I, as well as these,
   Grow lovely, growing old?

—*Karle Wilson Baker*

At left: There is something charming about this old and handsomely weathered store on the main road in Old San Simeon, California—in stark contrast to the opulence of the nearby castle of the same name built by the infamous William Randolph Hearst. *Above:* Also beautifully aged is this faded—but somehow more interesting for the fading—advertisement from a more genteel time, in Harmony, California.

184

HOME, SWEET HOME

'Mid pleasures and palaces though we may roam,
Be it ever so humble, there's no place like home!
A charm from the sky seems to hallow us there,
Which, seek through the world, is ne'er met with
    elsewhere.
  Home, home, sweet, sweet home!
    There's no place like home!

—*John Howard Payne*

Just as does the cute little girl *above*, we may well find that wherever we roam, we will always look toward home wherever that home may be —whether it be Newport, Oregon *(above)*, Rosemead, California *(below)* or Suisun, California *(right)*.

Below: This view of the corner of 4th and L streets in Eureka, California reveals Bob's Cafe, which is closed today but is usually open for breakfast. The fading but still strongly present old Victorian which is here seen a little ways back on L Street from the main drag, once housed one of the town's leading families. The times, they surely change.

188

A DAILY MIRACLE

June's sunshine on the broad porch shines
Through tangled curtains of crossing vines;
The restless dancing of the leaves
Dusky webs of shadow weaves,
That wander on the oaken floor,
Or cross the threshold of the door.
Scattered where'er their mazes run
Lie little phantoms of the sun:
Whatever chink the sunbeam found,
Crooked or narrow, on the ground
The shadowy image still is round.
   So the image of God in the heart of a man,
Which truth makes, rifting as it can
Through the narrow crooked ways
Of our restless deeds and days,
Still is His image—bright or dim—
And scorning it is scorning Him.

—*Edward Roland Sill*

Above: The old Shell station and its owner's house in Koloa, Hawaii, near Poipu Beach, on the sleepy southern coast of Kauai, shows the general design of the houses that line small Hawaiian main streets. A porch to shade against that sunshine is *de riguer*—though the church *at right*, located on a main street near the eastern end of the island of Molokai, is practically hidden in dense vegetation. *Below:* Hawaii State Highway 11 forms the main street for Kainaliu, on the island of Hawaii. Here, the Aloha Theater, the Aloha Cafe and the Aloha Village Store invite you in through their mutual porch—out of the main street sun.

from

CHRISTMAS IN CALIFORNIA

Can this be Christmas—sweet as May,
  With drowsy sun, and dreamy air,
And new grass pointing out the way
  For flowers to follow, everywhere?

Has time grown sleepy at this post,
  And let the exiled Summer back,
Or is it her regretful ghost,
  Or witchcraft of the almanac?

While wandering breaths of mignonette
  In at the open window come,
I send my thoughts afar, and let
  Them paint your Christmas Day at home.

For at the door a merry din
  Is heard, with stamp of feathery feet,
And chattering girls come storming in,
  To toast them at the roaring grate.

And then from muff and pocket peer,
  And many a warm and scented nook,
Mysterious little bundles queer,
  That, rustling, tempt the curious look.

Then, as the darkening day goes by,
  The wind gets gustier without,
And leaden streaks are on the sky,
  And whirls of evening are about.

Soon firelight shadows, merry crew,
  Along the darkling walls will leap
And clap their hands, as if they knew
  A thousand things too good to keep.

—Edward Roland Sill

At left and above: These two homes in northern California demonstrate that you don't need snow to celebrate Christmas, and it's not the decorations that matter either. Yet the flame which is represented by these electric lights was traditionally a candle, set in each household's window—to welcome the Holy Family into each home. On these main streets there will be room at the inn.